PEARLS

OF

WISDOM

"Again, the kingdom of heaven is like unto a merchant man, seeking goodly pearls: Who, when he had found one pearl of great price, went and sold all that he had, and bought it." – Matthew 13:45-46

THE ANOINTED WORD SERIES

EDGAR A. POSEY

TABLE OF CONTENTS

FOREWORD

It is my sincere desire that you approach this reading not merely as entertainment, but that you will allow the spiritual concepts and precepts presented here to take root and to lead you toward the change that God requires.

The book is a compilation of short passages, designed for easy reading and navigation to allow for quick access to specific topics. May the revelation of God light every page for you.

Above all, my prayer is:

> *"That the God of our Lord Jesus Christ, the Father of glory, may give unto you the spirit of wisdom and revelation in the knowledge of him..."*
> *– Ephesians 1:17*

Wisdom and Revelation will move you to higher heights and deeper depths in the Lord and will establish your faith in God – both now and in the world to come – world without end.

- Dr. Edgar A. Posey

YOU ARE YOUR WORST ENEMY!

"And of some have compassion, making a difference: And others save with fear, pulling them out of the fire; hating even the garment spotted by the flesh." – Jude 1:22-23

It is absolutely necessary for God to save you *from you*. You are *your biggest and worst enemy!* And, being saved is not difficult! What is difficult is attempting to be a "spiritual" human being. Being spiritual to a spiritual person is easy. Being spiritual is impossible for a human being because it is not possible for a human being to do what pleases God.

In salvation, flesh must die. Period. If you are not dead, you are not freed from sin. If you are not freed from sin, you are not saved. If you are not saved from you, you remain in your sin!

If Jesus had not died, there would be no salvation. How do you benefit from Jesus' death? You have to be dead with him; only then can you be resurrected with him. Jesus is looking for a people who will obey him and deny (be dead to) the flesh!

You must be dead to living after your flesh, which means you are dead to being controlled by the flesh. Mortify the deeds of the flesh so you can live spiritually. Speaking in tongues does not make you spiritual and neither can it save you! What saves you is obedience to the Lord. Anytime you allow flesh to control your life, you are in trouble!

PROSPER SPIRITUALLY

*"Wherefore let him that thinketh he
standeth take heed lest he fall."
- I Corinthians 10:12*

As a saved person, your life has become spiritual.
God, however, allows us to do things that are *legal*
in the fleshly realm. But, the fleshly mentality has
many of God's people bound. Many endanger their
spiritual life in salvation by becoming entangled in
flesh. Once you are brought to a state of
spirituality, it makes no sense to return to
following that which is natural.

*"There hath no temptation taken you but
such as is common to man: but God is
faithful, who will not suffer you to be
tempted above that ye are able; but will
with the temptation also make a way to
escape, that ye may be able to bear it."
– I Corinthians 10:13*

Because the Lord blessed you, don't take that to
mean that, now, you are standing – spiritually –
under your own power. Don't take credit from the
Lord. What the Lord did for you is what is causing
you to stand. It's about what the Lord has done to
get us to the place where we are able to serve him.
And, you cannot serve the Lord when you are
serving yourself. There is no shared custody!

What you have been tempted with is not something above and beyond what the Lord is able to deliver you from (or to bring you through). God would never allow a test to come to you that is above that which you are able to bear. He knows your capability. Sometimes, however, you are not willing to live up to your capability.

GROW SPIRITUALLY

"Knowing this, that the trying of your faith worketh patience." – James 1:3

It's the tests and trials in your life that promote spiritual growth. In Egypt, Pharaoh gave Israel difficult tasks, they multiplied and grew. When the tests come to your life, they are not coming to kill you, but to make you grow – spiritually.

The tests and trials are meant to build you up and strengthen you. Body builders use weights to build muscle. The way to build a muscle is to, first, tear it down.

But, we don't want to be torn down! We deceive ourselves by thinking that everything that comes to our life should be pleasant. We have the expectation that things should work the way we think they should work. With that mentality, you will never grow to be what God wants you to be.

You think you should have some measure of control over how your life progresses. But, what are you able to control? Absolutely nothing! The need to be in control of something is deception. We don't want to be at life's mercy! This thinking starts from childhood. It is frightening to some to think they are not in control. Man not only wants to control what he does, but also what others do. The fact is that it is God who is in absolute control.

MILK IS FOR BABIES

"And I, brethren, could not speak unto you as unto spiritual, but as unto carnal, even as unto babes in Christ."
– I Corinthians 3:1

Paul said to the Corinthians, "I could not talk to you about spiritual things because you only deal with things that are fleshly." They were conducting themselves as though they were newborn babes in Christ. Babies babble, drool and use the bathroom on themselves. And, that is acceptable for babies. It is not acceptable adult behavior!

Stop being fleshly minded! That is a tall order to give to one that is fleshly. The scripture is talking to you, the spiritual person, not you the fleshly person. You are to handle everything in salvation spiritually.

When you say, "Oops, I slipped up and said the wrong thing!" – then understand that what came out of your mouth did so because that is what is in abundance in your heart.

*"I have fed you with milk, and not with
meat: for hitherto ye were not able to bear
it, neither yet now are ye able."*
– I Corinthians 3:2

I fed you with milk not with meat. Milk is for
babies. They cannot chew meat. Babies are not
able to take strong teaching because they cannot
digest solid food.

There are people who have been in church for years
and the minute you start talking spiritually, it
hurts their feelings! "Don't give us that strong
food. Let us stay babies!"

*"For ye are yet carnal: for whereas there
is among you envying, and strife, and
divisions, are ye not carnal, and walk as
men?" – I Corinthians 3:3*

The person that is saved is not supposed to conduct
himself as a natural man. Do you cease being a
human being after you get saved? You must!
Being a human being means you operate by the
flesh and not the Spirit. You are now a spiritual
being.

How can envy and strife and division be in you if
you have the mind of Christ? Christ is not divided!
If we are saved, we should be speaking the same
thing.

Flesh does not want to give up. It tries to grasp every possible hope that it can to survive. As long as flesh is alive in you, you are spiritually dead! You will never serve God because flesh will always be in the way; in the flesh because you will always have a concern for your flesh.

DO THE RIGHT THING

"For while one saith, I am of Paul; and another, I am of Apollos; are ye not carnal?" – I Corinthians 3:4

Many are hurt because in all their trying, they are unable to make themselves do the right thing. If you want to do what is right, you are going to have to believe God. You cannot do it by human effort. Salvation is not one's ability to control himself. It is not self control!

We can always rationalize our wrong actions. We think if we say, "They made me mad," that is reasonable justification for our behavior. Once I get mad, I "clock out" from "saved" time. Then once I get over being mad, I "clock in" again! That is a trick!

"Who then is Paul, and who is Apollos, but ministers by whom ye believed, even as the Lord gave to every man?" – I Corinthians 3:5

There is someone through which every person has come to salvation. Sometimes that accounts for what a person believes. We are not to be concerned about who came and witnessed to us. The important thing is that we received salvation.

"Paul was more saved than Apollos!" "But, Apollos was a better speaker than Paul!" What difference does any of that make? Did you get saved? That is what is important!

WORK FOR THE LORD

"I have planted, Apollos watered; but God gave the increase." – I Corinthians 3:6

God desires to use you to win souls to the kingdom. We sometimes won't surrender ourselves to God so he can use us fully. You may witness to people continually and believe that you are planting seeds. But the scripture says that what you are doing amounts to zero! You can sow seeds all day long but if God does not give the increase, nothing will increase. And, it's not your seed, anyway! It's God's seed.

The important thing is that God is the one who gets all the glory and praise. It's not your glory – it belongs to God. You will get no reward according to what you did or did not perform. What have you reproduced since you came into salvation? What determines whether or not you have anything coming? How many souls have you brought to the Lord? "I've been busy. I have to look out for myself!"

God keeps a perfect record. Every man will receive his own reward according to his own work. Many are just too busy with their own personal lives. Make some time for the Lord's business. Witnessing is your job. It's your profession. Winning souls must take priority over everything!

"For we are labourers together with God: ye are God's husbandry, ye are God's building."– I Corinthians 3:9

If you are working with God, what you are doing has to be spiritual. God is a Spirit and when you are spiritual and working with God, you are going to bring souls in.

PROMOTE JESUS

"According to the grace of God which is given unto me, as a wise masterbuilder, I have laid the foundation, and another buildeth thereon. But let every man take heed how he buildeth thereupon."
– I Corinthians 3:10

In God, every person must take heed how he builds. The foundation is Jesus and everything we build on him has to be spiritual. It has to meet his specification – which is spiritual. If you start out building with metal, and then you say the metal is costing too much, and build the upper floor out of wood...you might have problems if the blueprint calls for metal.

Churches, today, are big and beautiful but many times they leave Jesus out! Church has become a social gathering or a Social Club. But, who is helping people, spiritually? That is the only thing that is important. Unless a person is spiritual, everything else you teach him cannot really benefit him.

The word is talking to people that are already saved. There is no need to tell people who are not saved what to do. The unsaved person will never be able to perform spiritual things. God can help anyone who will do what he tells them to do.

*"For other foundation can no man lay
than that is laid, which is Jesus Christ."
– I Corinthians 3:11*

The foundation is Jesus Christ. Everything is about and for Jesus. He is the foundation upon which your life is founded and is to be built.

If you attempt to push Jesus aside and do things other ways, to you, Jesus will become a rock of offense. Everyone who proclaims that they are promoting God but are misleading them because they are not teaching the truth, will have to answer to God.

We are the Lord's building. We are fitly framed together. We are rooted in him and we become ambassadors for Christ. We are to promote Jesus. What are you promoting?

If you are non-productive, what is your purpose? If a tree is not producing anything, it is hewn down and cast into the fire. It is time to start producing. Sometimes, we have too much excess and don't want to let those unnecessary attachments go. And we have a problem when God starts working on us to relieve us of the excess!

BUILD ON A SPIRITUAL FOUNDATION

*"Now if any man build upon this
foundation gold, silver, precious stones,
wood, hay, stubble;" – I Corinthians 3:12*

Would you ask the Lord – "Jesus, is it alright to
build gold upon your foundation?" What does gold
have to do with Jesus? The foundation is spiritual,
but is gold spiritual? No!

If you build gold, silver, etc. on a spiritual
foundation, how will those things stand? We deal
with what we consider to be valuable. We get
caught on those things of the world, believing that
the things of the world hold value. The most
valuable thing you can have is salvation.

Many consider gold to be valuable, but it is not
spiritual. You cannot build gold, silver, diamonds
or anything else on that which is spiritual. You
cannot use natural things to build spiritual things.

Many are trying to make salvation become
something other than spiritual. It is not of
monetary value and it is not something that is from
the earth.

The scripture tells us that everything will be tried
by the fire of testing. If you put gold, silver or
precious stone, wood or hay in fire, they will be

destroyed! The only thing that will not be burned up will be that which is spiritual.

SPIRITUAL WEAPONS

*"For the weapons of our warfare are not
carnal, but mighty through God to the
pulling down of strong holds;"*
– II Corinthians 10:4

The weapons of our warfare are not carnal. The
catchy things you may hear, such as "Kick the devil
out" or "Step on the devil's head!" are nothing but
junk if you're trying to do it by your own strength!

When the tests come that are intended to
strengthen you, you show your weakness by
yielding to your flesh – trying to fight spiritual
battles by fleshly means. You cannot defeat the
devil with carnal means. And, you cannot defeat
him by telling him off or commanding him!

The scripture says you must resist the devil! And
you cannot resist the devil unless you submit
yourself to God. If you don't submit yourself to
God, you will not be spiritual.

You cannot defeat the devil through carnal
methods. It is all done through the Spirit and by
what He has done.

HUMBLE YOURSELF BEFORE GOD

"For a certain woman, whose young
daughter had an unclean spirit, heard of
him, and came and fell at his feet:"
– Mark 7:25

This woman heard that Jesus was in the vicinity
and she came and fell down before him. She
humbled herself before him. She showed that he is
greater than she. Do you do that? Do you show the
Lord that you believe he is the greatest? Or are
you like Ali – believing that "I AM THE
GREATEST!"

You have to exalt the Lord and humble yourself.
Humility is making yourself of no reputation. You
are not promoting you. You are not trying to make
a name for yourself. When you are always trying to
prove to people that you are right, it is for the
purpose of defending yourself. Someone says
something to you and you start "running your
mouth" and trying to make them see what you
mean.

This woman had humility and she was willing to
humble herself and fall down at the feet of Jesus
and recognize his greatness. Trying to defend
yourself is of the flesh. Flesh wants to protect
itself. However, Jesus is the one who defends you –
you are not to defend yourself. You cannot do

anything with your flesh or about your flesh. You can't take care of you – that's God's job. Jesus is your defense. You don't need to defend yourself.

NO SUBSTITUTE FOR JESUS

"But Jesus said unto her, Let the children first be filled: for it is not meet to take the children's bread, and to cast it unto the dogs." – Mark 7:27

We are living in a day of substitutions – there are sugar substitutes, substitutes for salt, meat, butter, etc.... We substitute everything, including things for Jesus.

This woman believed the Lord could do what she asked. Most people would have been offended by what he said. "Who are you calling a dog?" But she was looking for something from the Lord. When you want something bad enough, you will not just accept "no" and go away. She said "Whatever is necessary, Lord; whatever you say!"

The Lord did not tell the woman "No." She was humble. She did not allow her flesh to flair up because she knew this was a life or death situation. This was about her daughter needing help.

If you believe God, what difference does it make when or how he does it? She kept herself under control. How easy is that to do? Someone does you wrong and you stay humble. If you get the victory, it will be because the Lord gave you victory. The more you can be kept out of the fight, the more chance you will have to see victory! Believe Jesus and don't accept any substitute because there is none!

STORMS COME TO ALL

"And there shall be a tabernacle for a
shadow in the daytime from the heat,
and for a place of refuge, and for a covert
from storm and from rain."
– Isaiah 4:6

Storms come to all, but the storms of life never
come to overthrow you. They come to bring you to a
place that God wants you to be.

You may feel "I don't see what is happening as
having anything to do with Jesus!"   But, who is it
that is trying to help you grow? The devil? No
way! God is trying to help you.

Do you ever think about this? Do you ever consider
God's will? You got saved to do his will and ever
since he saved you, what have you been doing?
Why come into salvation and serve yourself. That's
what you did before you were saved!

FAITH TO CHANGE

"Knowing this, that our old man is crucified with him, that the body of sin might be destroyed, that henceforth we should not serve sin." – Romans 6:6

Humans want to be in control. But, when you start trying to handle things, you create more problems for yourself. You show that you don't trust God when you do that. If you believe that God has taken care of the problem, you don't have a problem. You know it is in God's hand. You live spiritually, knowing that God has taken care of your physical and spiritual needs. It's already done!

The medical profession is getting rich because we trust in flesh – skin for skin. "I will pay and pay and pay to solve my problem!"
Many times you can tell others what to do; but, when it comes to your situation, you panic. If you won't believe God to be saved, what are the chances you will believe him for anything else? As soon as something happens that disagrees with your flesh, you don't like it and you react to it.

You're trying to believe God for something without being spiritual. What is the benefit of getting what you want from God if you are not saved? All the things you get will not console you in the lake of

fire! When you are saved, you have got to change!
You cannot just say "I accept that I am saved!" You
have to be saved and trust God for your salvation.
You must change!

WHO DO YOU LOVE?

*"So when they had dined, Jesus saith to
Simon Peter, Simon, son of Jonas, lovest
thou me more than these? He saith unto
him, Yea, Lord; thou knowest that I love
thee. He saith unto him, Feed my lambs."*
– John 21:15

Most people's problem is that they are more in love
with their flesh than they are with Jesus. Human
beings have a mind of their own and they mind the
things of the flesh – because they love their flesh!
As a human being, your next move is to try to
figure out how to control things. Rather than
accepting, by faith, that God is in control, you end
up missing what God has for you.

Faith is accepting what the Lord has already done.
Don't allow flesh to control you (flesh is controlled
by the devil!). Your flesh limits you. The only time
the limit is taken off is when you operate
spiritually. Operating spiritually is proof of your
love for the Lord!

DEAD TO LIVING AFTER FLESH

"And when he was come out of the ship, immediately there met him out of the tombs a man with an unclean spirit, Who had his dwelling among the tombs; and no man could bind him, no, not with chains..." – Mark 5:2–3

You must be dead to living after flesh in order to be saved. In fact, you must be delivered from the stronghold of flesh or you will be lost!

In the text, Jesus gets off the ship and is confronted by a wild man, a person who lives in the tombs. Something had to be wrong with him to want to live in a cemetery. Most people don't want to visit one much less live there among the dead.

He's not doing what he is doing of his own choice. He is not out there howling and cutting himself with stones just because he likes the pain. He is tormented. He is driven. Flesh is always a problem when it is in control of you! Stop living after the flesh and you won't have a problem with it.

"How do I get myself delivered from myself, by myself?" You can't! You must put your faith in the

Lord and accept what he has done. If you are going to get any help, you will get it by faith in the Lord!

FLESH IS OUT OF CONTROL!

"And always, night and day, he was in
the mountains, and in the tombs, crying,
and cutting himself with stones. But
when he saw Jesus afar off, he ran and
worshipped him..." – Mark 5:5-6

Here is a man who needs help! He is not satisfied
with being a mad man. When you find someone
acting crazy, don't think they just want to act like
that. He is under stress. Isn't it amazing that
nobody can bind him? No one is able to tame him
and he runs to Jesus, falls down and worships him!
This man is a "whacko" – but, he recognizes and
acknowledges Jesus! He knows a lot about Jesus,
also. The man's power source is coming from the
spirits that are in him. Jesus commanded the
unclean spirit to come out of the man.

"And he asked him, What is thy name?
And he answered, saying, My name is
Legion: for we are many." – Mark 5:9

A legion consists of 12,000. One person having that
many demons is out of control! How does this
happen to a person? Demons cannot operate in a
person that is spiritual. There has to be flesh that
is available.

Flesh wants to have its way all the time. It does not want to be denied. That's how you know it is flesh. Flesh says, "Don't make me suffer!"

Flesh is out of control! Jesus cast the legion out of the man and they entered into a herd of swine. After the demons entered the swine, they ran violently into the sea. If a pig doesn't want to be controlled by the devil, why do people? Because you are deceived into thinking that you are, somehow, in control!

FASTING AND PRAYING IS FOR YOU

"And he said unto them, This kind can come forth by nothing, but by prayer and fasting." – Mark 9:29

This kind can come forth by nothing but prayer and fasting. What does this mean? The point of prayer and fasting is not to make God do something, but to get you to the place where you need to be! Jesus said to them "Oh, faithless generation. How long shall I be with you?" He was saying, how long shall I suffer you or put up with you? Because you are not really getting the message!

They missed the key ingredient in salvation which is faith. Not *understanding*, but faith. You need to fast and pray if you are getting dull in faith and don't believe God the way you must.

People think fasting and praying will make God do something. But it is for you so that you will believe. So you don't have to say "Lord, help my unbelief." Reciting or just knowing the Word of God is not a substitute for having faith in it!

BENEFIT FROM THE LORD'S RESURRECTION

"And that he was buried, and that he rose again the third day according to the scriptures:" – I Corinthians 15:4

Not many benefit from the Lord's resurrection because they have not benefited from his death. Your flesh is alive and well! What is the purpose in resurrecting something that is alive?

When you are buried with Jesus and filled with the Holy Ghost, the old man was put to death. If he is now dead, how do you give him credit for being dead? You must conduct yourself at all times as him being dead. You reckon him to be dead!

You say, "I have these feelings, so, am I really dead?" You are dead. If you are not dead, you are not saved.

We have the "effeminate syndrome" – the problem of over exaggeration! A man who acts like he is a woman has a tendency (because he really does not know how a woman feels or acts) to overplay and exaggerate the role! His gestures and expressions tend to be over done!

If a person is now a spiritual being, but is trying to be an unsaved person, by his memory he will over

32

exaggerate. He becomes worse than he was before he got saved because he is trying to play a role from *memory*. He goes overboard!

You must first be put to death with Jesus – buried with him in his death. Only then you can be raised with him and benefit from his resurrection.

FROM EDUCATION TO SALVATION

"For by grace are ye saved through faith; and that not of yourselves: it is the gift of God: Not of works, lest any man should boast." Ephesians 2:8-9

It is difficult to help people in salvation because we want to do what we understand – "I have some human intelligence. I have some formal education!" That is what keeps you in trouble with God – using your understanding, intelligence and education instead of faith in him!

Many cannot make the transition from education to salvation. That which you know naturally is what keeps you in trouble spiritually. You keep fighting for yourself, defending yourself, trying to do something that you will never be able to do.

The believer experiences the gospel – the death, burial and resurrection of Christ. What is the purpose of the Bible always presenting the death, burial and resurrection of Christ? It is the message of salvation. If you do not follow what the message says, how will you get the benefit? How will you get what the Lord says you can have? Salvation has nothing to do with one's intelligence. All that is necessary is for one to "believe."

The message of salvation is that you must believe.
The gospel is that Jesus died, was buried and rose
again. Why do we need to know that? Because you
have to be dead and buried with him and you will
be resurrected to a new life! The Bible says that
baptism does now save us. Therefore, you must
accept that you are dead to living after your flesh.
You are dead with Christ." That solves the
problem!

WALK BY FAITH

"And when they looked, they saw that the stone was rolled away: for it was very great." – Mark 16:4

We look at a situation and say, "I cannot do this!" But if God tells you to do something, it will not be done by your effort, but by his. It is not your problem. You deal with it as though it is about what you have to do! That is the reason people are not saved and the reason the church is in such a sad state.

If you could go to heaven being the way you are (fleshly), the pastor could stop preaching and tell you whatever you want to hear! However, he must tell you what God tells him to tell you, even if you don't obey.

When you get through doing what you call praising God or worshipping God, does it change you? If you are not living saved, you do all those things and it won't change anything. Hell will still be your home!

WALK IN THE NEWNESS OF LIFE

*"So then they that are in the flesh cannot
please God. But ye are not in the flesh,
but in the Spirit, if so be that the Spirit of
God dwell in you. Now if any man have
not the Spirit of Christ, he is none of his."*
– Romans 8:8-9

Today, it's the "Money Cometh" gospel! It's the
"Kick the devil out!" gospel. We have gotten away
from being dead with Christ. We have gotten away
from being buried with him. And we have gotten
away from walking in the newness of life – which is
life in the Spirit.

We are dealing with salvation without the proper
understanding of the death, burial and
resurrection. What sense does it make to be put to
death and to be raised up to be the same person
you were? We are raised to the newness of life.
Changed. We are now spiritual beings, having the
power to live a spiritual life and be pleasing to the
Lord.

ACCEPT THE MIND OF GOD

*"For who hath known the mind of the
Lord, that he may instruct him? But we
have the mind of Christ."
– I Corinthians 2:16*

There are no human solutions to spiritual
problems. Trying to solve a spiritual problem with
natural means only makes it worse. As long as you
follow your way of thinking, you are openly
rebelling against God because you are telling him
he does not know how to run your life! You are the
worst enemy you have! Nobody thinks for you but
you. You make your decisions and you are
responsible for your actions and their
consequences!

Jesus is your husband – He is your head. Allow
him to tell you what you are to do and are not to do.
It is the nature of the human being to do wrong.
Doing wrong is comfortable to humans just as it is
comfortable for a dog to eat his vomit. When
humans do wrong, they are simply doing, like the
dog, what they are programmed to do. It's in your
DNA!

Now that we have gotten saved, God has given us
access to the mind of Christ and power to operate
by it.

ACCEPT WHAT GOD HAS DONE

"Let us hear the conclusion of the whole matter: Fear God, and keep his commandments: for this is the whole duty of man." – Ecclesiastes 12:13

People are looking for a way out of their dilemma. They are seeking satisfaction – but can't and will never find it in flesh!

King Solomon had one thousand wives and he was not happy. All the things that the world has to offer are vanity if God is not in control. Accept what God has done – that is where the real joy comes from.

People are still trying to have their way – even in salvation. They want people to agree with them and to allow them to do whatever they want. You will not have lasting joy because you will find that not all people will agree with you. Your happiness must lie in your commitment to serve the true and living God!

Nothing can stand in the way of your joy or peace when you commit to serving the Lord. If God said it, you have got to say "yes." However things are going, they are going God's way! He is in absolute control. He made a promise and all you have to do is accept it, by faith.

"Lord, everything you said is done and I am going to praise you for it! If you say I am delivered, blessed, etc., Lord, it is so! I will start operating the way you say I am."

God already made the promise and he will not take back what he has said. Your blessing is not tied to what you do in church. You are blessed because of your faith in what Jesus has promised you. Whatever he promises you can have, you will say "yes" with God. Stop arguing with him!

If God says you are blessed, get up and operate as someone who is blessed. We are trying to live on a human level – trying to handle things "down here." He has raised us to the spiritual level and now requires that we live there.

Stop cheating yourself! God is trying to make those things that he allows to come to make and shape and mold you. He is using pressure to make something better out of you. Put pressure on coal, coal becomes a diamond. Pressure on gold makes purer gold!

When you prune a tree, you are not trying to hurt the tree. You are trying to make it more productive. When God starts working on the stuff you need to get rid of, he is trying to get you ready. If you want to bear fruit for God, you have got to get rid of some of the stuff that is hanging on you.

PEOPLE ARE NOT YOUR PROBLEM

People are not your problem! When you have a problem with someone, God is trying to show you that you are living in the flesh. The Lord came to save you. When you are pure gold, fire will not make something else out of you. God is making you better than anything you have ever been. He is not trying to fix you up and cause you to be something you already were – only better! He is trying to make you something different.

Your praise should be: "Thank you for the tests and the trials, Lord, because when I come out on the other side, I will be victorious!" You can hold God to every promise that he has made and he will not take any one of them back!

We spend time trying to humanize what God has said. He is trying to get us ready to get out of here! You are trying to stay! Be ready when the Lord comes for *you*. Staying around here longer does not make you any closer to being ready.

LOVE THE LORD WITH A PURE HEART

"Now the end of the commandment is
charity out of a pure heart, and of a good
conscience, and of faith unfeigned."
– I Timothy 1:5

God does not intend for you to struggle in salvation.
When you struggle, it's because you are trying to
make things work for yourself. When you accept
what God has done for you, you can fulfill the
commandment by loving the Lord. You will do that
which God requires you to do simply because you
love him.

Love the Lord out of a pure heart – with no ulterior
motive or desire to get something for yourself.
"Lord, I serve you because I love you." Serve God
out of love for him whether he does anything more
for you or not. You must be willing to show him the
love you have for him.

"I'm not trying to get a new car or house. I'm not
trying to get you to work my finances out." When
you love the Lord, he will never let you "out do"
him! If you give God money, he will give you
money in return. And, he will give you more than
what you gave him!

If you cannot serve God when you are broke, you
won't serve him when you are rich. If you cannot

serve God without a mate, you won't serve him
when you have one. Operate in sincere faith. Faith
unfeigned.

PRAISE GOD IN THE TEST

When the temptation comes to have a problem with something, just begin to thank God for allowing the situation to help you become what you must for the Lord. Whatever comes, get ready to praise God; for the tests that you go through are designed to make you strong.

The Lord delivered you once and for all that you don't have to return to sin. You cannot serve God by the dictates of your flesh. God shows you where you live when you have a problem with the things that come against your flesh. You must live above tests and trials. No one can make you unsaved but you. It is your reaction to what others do that determines whether you are saved or not. God is fine tuning you – he's getting you ready to do a work for him.

LET GOD CONTROL YOU

In order to get your attention, there must be a
drastic move in your life when Jesus comes in!
Now that he is in your life, you must have a life to
manifest that he is in you. He will not dwell in an
unclean vessel.

God comes into your life to control you. If he is not
in control of you, your flesh is in control. When
flesh is in control, your life is out of control! Flesh
– which is destined for destruction – is not subject
to God!

Jesus came to deliver us from bondage to flesh so
we could operate in true faith. The just shall live
by faith. There are too many that believe in
themselves. They believe they can trust their
mind; however, operating according to their mind is
what causes them all sorts of problems.

Your mind will agree with your flesh! Therefore,
you are to operate by the direction of the Spirit of
God. The flesh and mind operate by sensory
perception – the five senses. The mind is
influenced by what it sees, hears, smells, tastes and
touches!

"How am I supposed to believe in something I
cannot see?"

We believe in many things we cannot see. You cannot see the cold germs that cause sickness. You cannot see the radio signals that allow you to hear sound over the airways. But you accept that these things exist. Faith in God requires the same type of acceptance. "I can't see it, Lord, but I accept that it just is!"

CHANGING YOU CHANGES EVERYTHING

"And Jesus answering said, Were there not ten cleansed? But where are the nine? There are not found that returned to give glory to God, save this stranger."
Luke 17:17-18

Some people start out wanting to know the Truth, but when they find out that following the Truth requires you to die out to flesh, they stop following after the Truth. You have to come to know that you are your worst problem. If you are the problem, then you are the solution to the problem!

Change you and you change everything. It is not someone else's fault – it's yours. God did not set it up that we would be hindered from becoming what we need to be because of someone else blocking us.

You are trying to maintain your humanness. But that's the problem. You say you want to get rid of your problem and at the same time, you are trying to hold on to you. Change you and you change everything!

THERE IS NO RESPECTABLE SIN

"To deliver such an one unto Satan for
the destruction of the flesh, that the spirit
may be saved in the day of the Lord
Jesus." – I Corinthians 5:5

How many think of bringing someone who is in sin
to the understanding that they are in sin? "Don't
say anything to them – you will drive them from
the church!"

How will you help them if they don't understand
that they are in sin? People justify what they do.
There is no justification in the word of God for sin;
but people justify it, nevertheless.

"We don't want them to leave. We don't want them
to feel bad!"

Why not? You want them to know they are wrong!
We are told that we have to deliver such a one to
Satan in order to get some help for them. I would
hope they would want you to help them. Evidently,
they are not seeing things clearly. They need
someone to get them back on the right track. They
have to know that if you commit sin, you are out of
the will of God.

We have made sin respectable. ("What you did is
not that bad!") But sin is sin. Jesus died a terrible

death because of our sin. Do you want the pastor to lie to you and say you are okay when you are not? When you stand before God, how will that help you? People think that just because one got baptized in the name of Jesus and filled with the Holy Ghost that they are saved, eternally! But we know better! Even if you have been baptized five times in the name of Jesus – if you are not living holy, you have no salvation!

PURGE THE LEAVEN

*"Your glorying is not good. Know ye not
that a little leaven leaveneth the whole
lump?" – I Corinthians 5:6*

A little leaven leavens the whole lump. Here's this
person who has committed sin and you walk
around glad you are not like him! Sometimes we
like to have someone like that in the congregation
so we can measure ourselves against them. But
that doesn't make you any "taller." Your glorying –
being glad you did not do what they did – is not
good.

That person in sin will contaminate other people.

"Brother So-N-So got away with it! He allowed
them to do it! So can I do it, too?" Just a little
yeast will leaven a whole lump of dough and
contaminate the entire peace of bread!

> *"Purge out therefore the old leaven, that
> ye may be a new lump, as ye are
> unleavened. For even Christ our passover
> is sacrificed for us:"*
> *– I Corinthians 5:7*

Purge the old leaven. Get rid of that which puffs
you up. If it puffs you up, then it is human-based.

It is fleshly. You must get rid of the old leaven that you may be a new lump.

How do you get rid of the old leaven? If you want unleavened bread you have to mix in more flour and not give it a chance to set and contaminate it. Sin operates the same way – a little goes a long way! It contaminates other people. And those people, in turn, contaminate others. You have to purge sin before it becomes a source of further contamination.

THE UNCOMPROMISED WORD

"Whereof I am made a minister according to the dispensation of God which is given me for you to fulfill the word of God." –
Colossians 2:5

It is your responsibility to present the word. You cannot dilute the word. You must not attempt to make the word more "palatable" or more acceptable. Why "water down" the message from God?

If you can accept it as a human being, it is not going to help you. It is supposed to be the way it is. It is supposed to be strong and it is supposed to be bitter.

You are not saved by whether you cut your hair, or wear make up. Obedience is the key! We are to minister and present the word of God. The word of God must be fulfilled. You are a minister of the word of God. Every time you talk to someone about the word, you are ministering the word of God.

NO FELLOWSHIP WITH SIN

*"I wrote unto you in an epistle not to
company with fornicators: Yet not
altogether with the fornicators of this
world, or with the covetous, or
extortioners, or with idolaters; for then
must ye needs go out of the world."*
– I Corinthians 5:9-10

Paul said I'm not telling you that you should not
accompany with the fornicators who are outside the
church! I am saying do not company with the
fornicators who are *in* the church because you
make them feel comfortable because you don't have
a problem with what they are doing!

If you had to stop companying with sinners who are
outside the church, you would have to go out of the
world...because that is what is in the world! Sin is
what sinners do. But saved people are not to sin!

Believers are not to fellowship with fornicators,
even those who are in the church. Yes, you can
witness and talk to those who are unsaved on your
job, at home, in your neighborhood. But, in the
church, you are not to have fellowship with those
who are sin. Fellowship breeds a sense of comfort
and undermines their need for making a real
change.

You have to get them to repent. If they don't
repent, they cannot be saved. You can give them
clothes, money, etc., but if they don't repent, they
still will not be saved. We have advocates of
sinners in the church ("Well, the church is the only
place where saints kill the wounded!") We are not
trying to kill them – we're trying to get them saved!
What will save them is the Truth!

PUT TO DEATH WITH JESUS

"For after that in the wisdom of God the world by wisdom knew not God, it pleased God by the foolishness of preaching to save them that believe."
– I Corinthians 1:21

You must be put to death with Jesus in order to be born again. A seed must be put into the ground in order for it to grow. Salvation is being dead to sin. We are to be dead to flesh because sin is in the flesh.

We want salvation to be something that "I" did. "I accepted the name! I remember the day and the time, and it was wonderful!"

But, what have you done since that time? People are stubborn. They refuse to accept that they do not always know what they think they know. This is one of the biggest problems in the church, today. Preaching is foolish to the world but it saves the believer!

The scripture does not say "them that *understand*." Being saved is for people who "believe." They called the early church "believers." They had to exercise faith in order to see the manifestation of the things of God. We want to get control of the things of God. It doesn't work that way. You must accept what God says, even when you cannot understand it. In fact, if you can understand it, it probably isn't God!

CHRIST, THE POWER OF GOD

*"But unto them which are called, both
Jews and Greeks, Christ the power of
God, and the wisdom of God."*
– I Corinthians 1:24

How is Christ the power of God? What is the power
for? How? What do you need power over? The
flesh. Can you have power over the flesh as long as
flesh is alive? No. God is the one that delivered us
from being fleshly. The power to not sin is in the
Spirit.

Most don't understand that. We feel it is up to us
to make ourselves do what we are supposed to do,
and then find out that we cannot do it.

The Lord brings power to us to be able to live a
sinless life. You cannot live sinless as long as you
are living by the flesh. As long as flesh controls
you, you are going to sin.

The power comes from you being put to death with
Jesus. If you are not dead with Christ, then you
have no power over your fleshly life to be saved.
You will continue living a fleshly life; yet confessing
that you are saved. If you are not dead with Christ,
you have no power.

The foolishness of God is wiser than men. When you accept Jesus, you have both the power of God and the wisdom of God.

But, you continue to think that your feelings, knowledge, human experience, intuition, mother-wit, etc. count for something! But all of those things are neutralized in salvation. You are no longer a human being. You are a spiritual being. Old things are passed away.

Power comes because you are dead with him. You don't have physical power, but you have spiritual power. You are one with Jesus and the power that he has is now your power! When you do things independent of the Lord, you are operating outside the Power Source!

GOD IS CALLING

"Because the foolishness of God is wiser than men; and the weakness of God is stronger than men." – I Corinthians 1:25

This is not saying that God is foolish or preaching is foolish. But, it means that to the natural man, God and preaching do not make sense. No man has been able to figure out how to save a man – or cure leprosy. The things that men cannot do, God can do. The foolishness of God is wiser than the wisdom of men! The weakness of God (if he had any) would still be stronger than men.

Man's focus and destiny is to be spiritual. But, tragically, he falls in love with his flesh. God says, "I've got something better for you!" We say, "I am in no rush to get it. I live fleshly as long as I possibly can!"

"For ye see your calling, brethren, how that not many wise men after the flesh, not many mighty, not many noble, are called:" – I Corinthians 1:26

God does not call those who are already of reputation. It's too difficult to deflate them! He gets people who are already deflated so he can put in them what he wants. Humans want to feel that they know something. When a person thinks they know something, they are not open to be taught. You cause yourself to miss out on the things God has in store for you because you will not do things God's way (spiritually). You cannot change one thing that God has set in motion. "Let's go on a fast. Let's have a prayer vigil. We are going to change God's mind!" Not so – those things are meant to change you. God never changes!

SPIRITUAL THINGS ARE FOOLISH TO THE WORLD

*"But God hath chosen the foolish things
of the world to confound the wise; and
God hath chosen the weak things of the
world to confound the things which are
mighty." – I Corinthians 1:27*

Spiritual things, to the world are foolish! The
world cannot know spiritual things. "You mean
you give that much money in tithes and offerings to
the church!?" To the world, that is pure
foolishness!

But, to you, it will be a blessing. Your biggest
problem is that you will not obey. You already
think you know something of value – that is what
keeps you from obeying! You've been doing the
same thing the same way all these years and it has
not worked for you yet. But you keep trying!

The things that God ask you to do are outside of
your ability to accomplish. They have to be –
otherwise, you would find a way to take credit from
God! God has taken those things that you consider
to be powerless and he uses them to bring down
great empires. Because of faith, it works – so that
you can learn that it is not about power or might of
the world. It is about faith in God. God is in

absolute control of everything. We sometimes feel that the devil has some things he can control. But, he also is under the control of God! He cannot do anything that God does not give him the "ok" to do.

INHERIT THE KINGDOM

*"Know ye not that the unrighteous shall
not inherit the kingdom of God? Be not
deceived: neither fornicators, nor
idolaters, nor adulterers, nor effeminate,
nor abusers of themselves with mankind,
nor thieves, nor covetous, nor drunkards,
nor revilers, nor extortioners, shall
inherit the kingdom of God."*
– I Corinthians 6:9–10

Nothing you did caused you to get saved. No one
can boast of who they were as a human being. As a
human, you were nothing but a depraved sinner.
That is a difficult concept for people to believe.
Humans want to believe "I am somebody!"

Telling yourself that you are somebody does not
make you somebody. It's not you that is important.
It is what is *in* you that makes you important. The
container is not important, but what is in the
container. We have accepted the death, burial and
resurrection of the Lord and that allows us to
benefit from the work at Calvary.

When we are not living after flesh, we cannot be
fleshly beings – we become spiritual beings. You
must be dead to your flesh to be saved. If you are
not dead to flesh, that should cause you some

concern. Do you convince yourself that you are still saved even though you are not dead to your flesh?

Do you not know that the unrighteous will not inherit the kingdom of God? What do you consider unrighteous? What do you consider sin? People who engage in sin will not go to heaven!

CREATED TO BE SPIRITUAL

"And such were some of you: but ye are
washed, but ye are sanctified, but ye are
justified in the name of the Lord Jesus,
and by the Spirit of our God."
– I Corinthians 6:11

Some of us have a reviling spirit. Sometimes,
before a word can get out of someone's mouth, you
are defending yourself! It is the Lord's job to
defend you. Flesh has to be dead if you are going to
be saved.

You are washed. You have been cleansed from the
filth of the flesh – purified from a life in the flesh.
If you continue to live after the flesh, even though
you have been baptized in the name of Jesus and
filled with the Holy Ghost, you are still a sinner.
Sin is in the flesh! The Lord has justified you just
as if you had never done wrong. You are not
justified by anything that you would be able to do.

You think you got saved because you tarried and
said all those "thank you, Jesus." We have people
thinking that once you speak in tongues, that's it!
But, the new birth comes to change you. Did you
change? It does more than just give you the ability
to speak in another language!

You have taken on a spiritual life. Some people
love being a human being and are stuck on being
human. But being human was simply an
intermediate stage, much the same way a
caterpillar is the intermediate stage for a butterfly;
or a tadpole is the intermediate stage for a frog.

God never intended for us to remain humans. We
were created to be spiritual beings and to do
spiritual things!

FLESH LOVES THE EASY WAY

"Meats for the belly, and the belly for meats: but God shall destroy both it and them. Now the body is not for fornication, but for the Lord; and the Lord for the body." – I Corinthians 6:13

We want to nail salvation down to a thing – what you wear, what you don't wear, etc... But you have a bigger problem than what you are wearing or pulling off. We think salvation has to do with works – what we do or do not do. You cannot grow spiritually unless you are spiritual, no more than a dog can grow to be a human! You have to have the "DNA" of a spiritual being to grow spiritually.

Flesh, which has no "spiritual DNA," loves the easy way! It loves what it thinks is easy. "Meats for the belly and the belly for meats." Carnal things are what the body desires. A fleshly person desires those things that are of the flesh. That is what they look for. That is their interest. You can deal with something spiritually and they will always bring it around to what is human. Fleshly people want to humanize those spiritual things that you present.

Flesh is going to be destroyed – it did not come here to last forever. If you build all your hopes and dreams upon your flesh, you waste your time here on earth. God has something better for his people. We get stuck on meat – "It's all about my flesh! I want everything to make my flesh comfortable and happy!"

God shall destroy both it and them. The body is not for sin; sin is a problem of the flesh. The body is for the Lord. Do that which pleases the Lord for your body because your relationship with him is spiritual.

DEATH HAS NO POWER

*"And God hath both raised up the Lord,
and will also raise up us by his own
power." – I Corinthians 6:14*

The Lord has been raised up and he will also raise
us up by his power. This is the same power that
raised Jesus from the dead. Our life comes from
being dead with Christ. We shall also live with
him. Once you get saved, death has no power over
you. You now live by faith in God and not by what
happens in the flesh. You operate by faith in what
the Lord has done. Life is not about what we
originally thought it was about and the change in
us is not by anything that we can do.

*"Know ye not that your bodies are the
members of Christ? Shall I then take the
members of Christ, and make them the
members of an harlot? God forbid."
– I Corinthians 6:15*

Your body is a member of Christ. You belong to
Jesus. You are a part of him and he is a part of
you! You must not take that which belongs to
Jesus and attempt to become joined to a harlot.
The Lord will never become part of what we are as
fleshly beings.

"What? know ye not that he which is joined to an harlot is one body? for two, saith he, shall be one flesh."
– I Corinthians 6:16

The physical relationship to which you are joined in marriage, the twain shall become one flesh. The Lord took Eve out of Adam and then gave Eve back to Adam. The person to which you are joined in the body is one flesh – with you. You cannot be joined in a relationship with someone and not be what they are.

LIVING FOR FLESH BRINGS BONDAGE

*"But he that is joined unto the Lord is
one spirit." – I Corinthians 6:17*

If you are joined to a harlot, you and the harlot are
one. When you join yourself to Christ, you become
one with him. How, then, can you operate
independently of him? "I am my own person.
Nobody tells me what to do!"

You are one spirit with him, not one body. A
spiritual being is not seeking to commit sin.
Humans get caught up in trying to gratify their
flesh. You are supposed to be living a life by the
direction of the Spirit.

*"Flee fornication. Every sin that a man
doeth is without the body; but he that
committeth fornication sinneth against
his own body." – I Corinthians 6:18*

Flee fornication! Everything else you do that is sin
is without the body. If you lie on someone, that is
outside the body. You are doing something to
someone else. When you commit fornication, you
sin against your own body. If you are taking that
which belongs to the Lord and using it for
fornication, you are taking yourself out of the
spiritual realm and entering into the operation of
flesh, once again.

71

If you don't realize what you are doing to yourself, you are going to self destruct and end up in the lake of fire. Flee fornication. Get away from it. If you have salvation, you better hold on to it! That's the only thing that really counts. Don't place yourself back into bondage and break your spiritual relationship with the Lord. Living for your flesh brings bondage.

GLORIFY GOD IN YOUR BODY

*"What? know ye not that your body is the
temple of the Holy Ghost which is in you,
which ye have of God, and ye are not your
own?" – I Corinthians 6:19*

If your body is the temple of the Holy Ghost, how
can you use it for sin? Would you sin in heaven?
Ye are not your own. Why do people think they
belong to themselves? "I thought we could choose
some things!"

What you choose is probably the wrong thing.
Flesh is unable to make rational choices. The Lord
has to make your choices – it's not up to you. We
grow up living under fairy tales. You want to find
your mate, and the two of you ride off into the
sunset and live happily ever after. Don't forget
about the one you belong to and what he wants you
to do. We still think that some of our time belongs
to us.

*"For ye are bought with a price: therefore glorify
God in your body, and in your spirit, which are
God's." – I Corinthians 6:20*

You are bought with a price. What was the price of
your salvation? The death of Jesus Christ; and you
are to be dead with him. What does it cost you for
salvation? Your life! It is free because you don't

have to physically be dead. You did not have to pay
that penalty for yourself. It is free from you having
to pay the penalty of the law, being dead with
Christ. He paid the penalty for you with his life.
He died in our stead so we could be dead with him.
Glorify God in your body because your body and
your spirit belong to God. Don't take that which
belongs to him and use it as an instrument of sin.
Use it to his glory!

DELIVERANCE FROM THE ENEMY

*"Moreover, brethren, I would not that ye
should be ignorant, how that all our
fathers were under the cloud, and all
passed through the sea."*
– I Corinthians 10:1

In the wilderness, the Jews experienced a type of
baptism. They had a form of salvation presented to
them in their deliverance from the enemy. There
are not too many of you, today, who are concerned
about being delivered from the enemy, are there?
Especially since the enemy is you! If you are not
delivered from you, you are not delivered!

Something psychological is going on in your mind
that keeps you from accepting that you could be
your own worst enemy. Who creates problems for
you? Who causes you to deal with things the way
you do? If you sought direction from the Lord, he
would not direct you to handle things the way that
you do.

What is described in the scripture above is the
"baptism of Moses." They were all under the cloud
– which was water and they were all in the sea,
which was water. They were surrounded by water
which is a form of baptism. The ones who passed
through the sea all received the same baptism. The
sea was red. Because of the clay that was in that

area, it was tinted by the clay. The color "red"
represented the blood – or death. That is how a
person is saved – by being put to death. We are to
be buried with Jesus.

THE SPIRITUAL ROCK

*"And did all drink the same spiritual
drink: for they drank of that spiritual
Rock that followed them: and that Rock
was Christ." – I Corinthians 10:4*

The Spiritual Rock that followed them was Christ!
Did he exist before he was born of Mary? If he
followed them in the wilderness, he had to have
existed!

*"But with many of them God was not well
pleased: for they were overthrown in the
wilderness." – I Corinthians 10:5*

He set all this up to show us the problem. They all
benefited from what the Lord did. "As long as God
is doing the blessing, I am okay until he starts
placing requirements on me! I am used to him
giving to me, but I don't want him to require
anything of me! When he does, I am ready to leave
him!"

With many of them, God was not well pleased and
they were overthrown. What happens to these
people who are getting all these spiritual benefits
now that they are there in the wilderness? As soon
as the tests come, they fall away from being
"spiritual."

"Now these things were our examples, to the intent we should not lust after evil things, as they also lusted."
– I Corinthians 10:6

The intent is that we should not lust after evil things. Evil here means "fleshly'. Don't convince yourself that you are saved just because you were baptized in the name of Jesus and spoke in tongues. The Lord did all of this for them and when their flesh was tested, they failed. When God requires you to deny yourself of something, you must be willing to go through what he requires.

GENETIC PRE-DISPOSITION

*"Neither be ye idolaters, as were some of
them; as it is written, The people sat
down to eat and drink, and rose up to
play." – I Corinthians 10:7*

They took that with which God had blessed them
and they ate and drank and, then, decided "We're
full – it's time to play!" They were having a party
when Moses came down out of the mountain and
they had started worshipping the golden calf that
they had made! They said "This be the god that
brought us out!"

What is wrong with the human mind? You know
something is not correct and you cause yourself to
believe in spite of what you know is right. Does it
make any difference that God did all these things
for them? God has proven that doing things for
people does not change them. The minute you do
something they don't like, they are going to turn
against you!

*"Neither let us commit fornication, as
some of them committed, and fell in one
day three and twenty thousand."
– I Corinthians 10:8*

23,000 people fell in one day! But, they all came
through the red sea, baptized unto Moses, ate the

spiritual food and drank the spiritual drink. But, with many of them, God was not pleased. When they were put to the test, they went right back to serving their flesh. God wants us to know as long as we allow flesh to control us, we will serve ourselves. You will never get flesh to stop serving self. It is in it's seed – it's DNA – to serve itself!

THE CONSEQUENCES OF COMPLAINING

"Neither let us tempt Christ, as some of them also tempted, and were destroyed of serpents." – I Corinthians 10:9

The people of God tempted Christ in the wilderness. They murmured and complained. And the Lord allowed fiery serpents to come out and bite the people and many of them died. Does knowing this stop us from murmuring and complaining, today? When you are complaining, who are you complaining against? The problem is you are not submitting yourself to God and you are asking God to do something for you unreasonably.

We have this false understanding that just because I say that God is going to take care of something, that he will! "I don't serve him and I don't trust him any other time, but, in this instance, I believe him and expect him to come through for me!" Don't tempt Christ.

Don't keep murmuring and complaining against him. You don't like what you are causing in your life and you blame it on the Lord. Yet, you created the problem because you did not do it the way God said do it. It seems easier to deal with foolishness than deal with sound doctrine. And the devil has you neutralized – he has destroyed you because you cannot get any help!

ADMONISHED BY GOD

"Neither murmur ye, as some of them also murmured, and were destroyed of the destroyer." – I Corinthians 10:10

It is not good to murmur against the Lord. If you don't like the way something is going, keep it to yourself! A lot of things that happen will work to keep your mind off the Lord. We have become convinced that life is what I do and how I work things out and we fail to accept what God has already worked out.

Since there are things in the scripture written for our admonition, why don't people want to be admonished? How do you benefit from the things that God gives to admonish you, if you are never admonished by them? "You are belittling me. You are putting me down! I don't like to be talked down to!"

People don't like to be told anything. You might as well receive the Truth so you can get some help. Line up with the word and be blessed. Or, keep doing what you do and suffer the consequences. You cannot blame anyone else for what happens in your life because God has given you an opportunity to follow him. God wants to inform you – to admonish you. There are certain things you must follow!

"I got the Holy Ghost just like you! I don't need anyone telling me what to do!"

It is for your admonishment. The end time is now. We are living in the end time. You know there is not a lot of time left. Be admonished, today!

AGREE WITH YOUR ADVERSARY – QUICKLY

"Agree with thine adversary quickly,
whiles thou art in the way with him;" –
Matthew 5:25

When the tests come and we complain, we are
accusing God of being unjust. Some of you, because
of stubbornness and being stiff-necked, you will go
through a lot because God has got to make you
pliable if you are going to make it to heaven. Agree
with your adversary quickly!

When adversity comes, agree with it. If you are
floating in a body of water and the current is strong
and it is trying to take you down the stream,
surrender to the water. The water will take you to
where the water is calm. Otherwise, you will fight
and wear yourself out and drown!

The Lord has everything taken care of. When you
trust him, you are blessed. God knows what it
takes to make you what you need to be. Surrender.
"Okay, Lord, have your way!" If your life doesn't
change, it doesn't mean a thing!

God did not come to make us a little better. He
came to change us – completely! He will make a
way of escape. And this is where we stop – on the

word "escape." But God's way of escape is that you may be able to bear it! So, bear it!

"Okay, if that is my lot, I will do and go on about my business!" And before you know it, the test is over!

WITHOUT PREPARATION

"Glorious things are spoken of the, O city of God. Selah" – Psalm 87:3

There are many things spoken of about the city of Zion. But if you do not allow God to save you, all the talking you do is of no importance. By us being dead with him, we are resurrected to new life...not just made better. But we love being human even with all the misery and problems it causes. What will happen when you leave here? No preparation means you are not going to spend an eternity with God. You would not think that a person could become so stuck on themselves that they are willing to spend eternity in hell. This does not make sense, does it?

"I will make mention of Rahab and Babylon to them that know me: behold Philisitia, and Tyre, with Ethiopia; this man was born there. " – Psalm 87:4

This is why Mt. Zion is of such great importance – the birth of Jesus Christ. It's also the place of the death, burial and resurrection of Jesus, so it encapsulates the salvation plan. But we are not looking to be dead. We are hoping that, somehow, salvation will include possessing the things of this world.

You are to deny living after your human will that you might live by the Spirit of God. There are greater blessings in the Spirit of God than anywhere else. The trick of the devil is that you hold the key to your happiness. He knows you will never find it and you will eventually give up trying and go back to living after flesh. Victory is in the new life, being dead to flesh, serving God. There is life after death. It is not a pretend life. Prepare for it!

YOUR REASONABLE SERVICE

"Or saith he it altogether for our sakes? For our sakes, no doubt, this is written: that he that ploweth should plow in hope; and that he that thresheth in hope should be partaker of his hope."
– I Corinthians 9:10

God said these things for our sake and for the sake of the ministry. Not because of concern for oxen. When you give to the ministry, it will bless the ministry and you. You will be partaker of the hope. What you do for the Lord, he is going to bless you for it. Never hold out on your giving because you don't agree with what the preacher is saying. You will hurt no one but yourself!

> *"I beseech you therefore, brethren, by the mercies of God, that ye present your bodies a living sacrifice, holy, acceptable unto God, which is your reasonable service." – Romans 12:1*

You believe what the Lord has done and you receive the blessing. The Lord blesses us so that we will be more excited about serving him. The Levites were supported by the other tribes. They were not given an inheritance the way the others were. They offered spiritual service to the other tribes. The Lord showed that this is his way of supporting those who are ministering spiritual things.

BE COMPLETE IN GOD

*"Now concerning the things whereof ye
wrote unto me: It is good for a man not to
touch a woman." – I Corinthians 7:1*

His divine plan for marriage involves a man and a
woman – living together joyfully. This has nothing
to do with you and your preferences. The purpose
is for you to carry out the will of God. You are to
promote his purpose. He wants you to do things for
the benefit of the Lord that are not necessarily
pleasing to you. If you and your spouse are living
for the Lord, you both ought to be completely
happy. Many will say I am not going to get
married – but they end up fornicating! Let every
man have his own wife and every woman her own
husband. Don't pretend that you are so spiritual
while you are "slippin' and slidin'" – get your own
wife or husband!

*"Let the husband render unto the wife
due benevolence: and likewise also the
wife unto the husband." – I Corinthians
7:3*

You are not in control of anything. The wife and
husband have no power over their own bodies. God
is the one that controls. If you have a problem,
appeal to God. If you don't let him take care of the
situation, then you cannot blame him for the

problem not being resolved. Not giving it to God means that you think you are tough enough to handle it yourself. And God will let you do just that!

God has provided for the church everything it needs. God is a Spirit, but we are not looking for what is spiritual. We are looking for things that make life easier in the flesh. And, therefore, we have a problem. You never have to backslide, get in the flesh, etc. to get anything spiritual taken care of. God has given us everything we need.

PUT *YOU* OUT OF YOUR LIFE!

*"Now concerning spiritual gifts, brethren,
I would not have you ignorant. Ye know
that ye were Gentiles, carried away unto
these dumb idols, even as ye were led."
– I Corinthians 12:1–2*

When you know something does not work, but you
keep doing it, isn't that an indication of a mental
problem? It has been said that insanity is doing
things the same way and expecting different
results! Some people think the Jews had favor with
God. They were given the knowledge, but they did
not use it. They were no better off than the
Gentiles because they did not obey God.

Being led by human will is what gets people in
trouble. Doing what is fleshly is easier than doing
spiritual things because you have to deny self to be
spiritual. If you desire to please the Lord, however,
you won't live for your flesh. A person does not
know that Jesus is Lord except by the revelation of
the Holy Spirit. Many people say that Jesus is
Lord, but they don't live a life unto him. "He is the
One on the throne running my life." If that is true,
what are you doing making decisions?

You make determinations to change. "I know I need
to do something but I end up doing nothing!" You
must put you out of your life! Stop dealing with

things according to your thinking – your likes, dislikes, don't wants, etc. – all that you are trying to make happen, God has already done!

LINE UP WITH GOD'S AGENDA

*"But the manifestation of the Spirit is
given to every man to profit withal."*
– I Corinthians 12:7

You do not line up with God's agenda because you
have your own. You think yours is workable and
you fail to line up with the Lord's. You never give
up on you. You continually try to make things
succeed for you!

God does not change his plan and do something for
some other purpose other than salvation. Did Jesus
die just so you could have a new automobile? A
mate? A new house? If God blessed some of us with
the things we want, there would be no way that he
would be able to save us! Salvation is spiritual. If
your spiritual life is on track, everything else falls
in place. There is no "pill" for your spiritual
problem! The key is faith.

How do you get past having an agenda? Your
agenda didn't work when you had it in the world.
Now that you have come into salvation, you cannot
make it work. The Lord has already worked
everything out in behalf of the church. Why not
accept it? When you are being given spiritual
information and you try to take it in through the
five senses, you are trying to make things work

through your human effort. Cease from operating by flesh and line up with God's agenda. Lining up with God is the only guarantee you have of victory.

SPIRITUAL HELP

"For to one is given by the Spirit the word
of wisdom; to another the word of
knowledge by the same Spirit;"
– I Corinthians 12:8

The Lord, by the Spirit, gives you a word of
wisdom. It is not from you. Don't get puffed up. It
is the Lord. It is not about you. You didn't have
the gift when you were born. If the Holy Spirit has
manifested this gift in you, it was spiritually done –
it was an operation of the Spirit. These gifts are
given to build up the church – to help the church to
accomplish what the church has been put into the
world to do, which is to bring souls into salvation.
Winning souls is your profession. It's your calling –
wherever you are…on the job, in your
neighborhood, or at the grocery store…wherever.

"To another faith by the same Spirit; to
another the gifts of healing by the same
Spirit;" – I Corinthians 12:9

The Holy Spirit manifests all the gifts. They are
operated by the self same Spirit. The gift of faith is
not the same as having faith. The gift of faith
means one has the ability to believe against all
odds! It is divinely imparted for a specific spiritual
purpose. However, everybody who is going to be

saved must walk by faith – not by their human
ability or understanding. It is not something that
you, of your own human effort, can produce.

GIFTS ARE GIVEN TO PROFIT ALL

"To another the working of miracles; to another prophecy; to another discerning of spirits; to another divers kinds of tongues; to another the interpretation of tongues..." – I Corinthians 12:10

Isn't it strange that some of these gifts are seldom used, although the prophetic gifts are overworked? Discerning of spirits – refers to the gift to distinguish whether a message or action that is going forth is of the Spirit of God or the devil. The scripture says believe not every spirit; but to try the spirit by the Word. The devil is not going to back up the Word. He is trying to tear down and discredit it!

"But all these worketh that one and the selfsame Spirit, dividing to every man severally as he will." – I Corinthians 12:11

The same Spirit works all these gifts – dividing to every man severally as he will. God can use you in any gift that he wants to as long as you are submitted to the Spirit. One person does not have to just have one gift. The gifts are given to profit all – not just for you to profit. You don't know how blessed you could be if you accepted what the Lord says. You are still trying to operate according to the flesh. It is great to talk about the sacrifice that was paid for our redemption. Most people do not know what that means or how it benefits us. What the Lord's death did for us is not understood.

It is not accepted in the manner in which it should be. We are now coming to a little better understanding about how we come to have salvation. We find out that what has been taught for many years is not what the Bible is teaching, at all. This is acceptable to some because it seems to be easier if we just "claim" that we are saved!

THE CARNAL MAN IS HANDICAPPED FROM BIRTH

"After the same manner also he took the cup, when he had supped, saying, This cup is the new testament in my blood: this do ye, as oft as ye drink it, in remembrance of me."
– I Corinthians 11:25

Man has a serious problem. He has learned how to *play* being saved. But, when the pressure comes, what's really inside comes out! It would be easier to change a man if he did not have so much pride in *his* ability to change things. Although he doesn't have the ability; he does not realize it! Jesus took the cup, sipped it, and passed it on to the disciples and admonished them to do this, whenever they commune, in remembrance of him.

The point to remember is that you died with Jesus. How often do you think about that? The part that you have with him is spiritual. He came so we could have a different kind of life than we already had. God's plan is not for human beings. You are still a human being if you are *playing* the role of one that is saved. But, you must get off the "stage" and accept what you really are in Christ – that is, a spiritual being.

"For as often as ye eat this bread, and drink this cup, ye do show the Lord's death till he come. Wherefore whosoever shall eat this bread, and drink this cup of the Lord, unworthily, shall be guilty of the body and blood of the Lord."
– I Corinthians 1:26-27

You do this in remembrance, reminding yourself that you are dead with Jesus. It behooves you to get your life together. People think the solution to their problem is not to participate in communion. But, if you are not right with the Lord, you are still in trouble, whether you take communion or not!

EXAMINE YOURSELF

"But let a man examine himself, and so let him eat of that bread, and drink of that cup." – I Corinthians 11:28

Examine yourself so you might know where you really are. Make sure you are not a reprobate! Many take communion with unconfessed sin because they want people to think they are okay. Why are you no more concerned about your salvation than you are? You hope that when you get to heaven that Jesus will be playing the same game you are playing, right? God forbid!

"For he that eateth and drinketh unworthily, eateth and drinketh damnation to himself, not discerning the Lord's body. For this cause many are weak and sickly among you, and many sleep." – I Corinthians 11:29–30

This is not talking about someone who, through some effort they have made, is worthy. You are accepting that you are worthy because you accept what Jesus has done for you. He died for you. This is not human worthiness. Accepting what Jesus has done, he died and you are dead with him. You are dead to living after your flesh. Do you not know what Jesus purchased for us when he went to the cross? Many are sick and many are asleep because they did not know what the Lord did for us. We are no longer bound to sin. Flesh keeps saints from fulfilling their commitment to serve the Lord. Human beings are not designed to do good. They are designed to do evil. There is no good thing in the flesh!

SOUNDING BRASS

*"Though I speak with the tongues of men
and of angels, and have not charity, I am
become as sounding brass, or a tinkling
cymbal." – I Corinthians 13:1*

If a person is playing taps, but not sounding the
right note, military people won't know what to do.
If it is not making a familiar sound, there is
confusion. Likewise, when you are speaking the
word but you don't have love, it means nothing. It
becomes sounding brass – just making noise.

*"And though I have the gift of prophecy,
and understand all mysteries, and all
knowledge; and though I have all faith,
so that I could remove mountains, and
have not charity, I am nothing."
– I Corinthians 13:2*

"I am able to prophesy at will and have all
knowledge and know all kinds of stuff and have all
faith that moves mountains, but if I don't have love,
I am nothing!" Why? Because you are still a
human being if you don't have the "agape" love –
love in spite of. God does not love people because of
what they look like or what they do. His love is not
conditional. If you love someone because of what

they look like, for instance, as soon as that changes, your love is gone!

LOVE IS KIND

"Charity suffereth long, and is kind;
charity envieth not; charity vaunteth not
itself, is not puffed up," – I Corinthians
13:4

Charity is still kind even after suffering. "I have
endured this person all this time. I am at my wits
end!" It suffers long and is still kind. Charity is
not envious of other people's blessings. Charity
does not vaunt itself. It is not self–exalting. If you
love, you don't exalt yourself. It is not puffed up. It
does not make itself important.

> *"Doth not behave itself unseemly, seeketh*
> *not her own, is not easily provoked,*
> *thinketh no evil." – I Corinthians 13:5*

Charity does not behave itself unseemly. It seeks
not her own, which means one cannot always be
concerned about what he wants! It is not easily
provoked, which means that you can pick at her all
day and she won't get mad. Not "touchy." Love
thinks no evil. ("Yeah, he did that because he
doesn't like me.") Love never becomes inflated with
its own ego. It never makes itself of great value.

> *"Rejoiceth not in iniquity, but rejoiceth in*
> *the truth." – I Corinthians 13:6*

Love doesn't get happy about sin, or revel in the fact that another has sinned. ("Trying to pretend you are so holy! Now you are in trouble. You're just like the rest of us!") But it rejoices in the truth. It is hearing the truth that makes you happy, even though it may hurt. It is in facing the truth that one will seek God's help to make a change. Indeed, the truth does make one free.

GOD'S BODY IS SPIRITUAL

"Now ye are the body of Christ, and members in particular." – I Corinthians 12:27

Everyone in the body has a part to play. We need to be in position to be of help to win people to Christ. There are many trying to perform and do their part in the body of Christ when they are not even in the body! That creates a great problem. When you are not in the body, how do you do something in the body of Christ?

People deal with their spiritual relationship with the Lord as though it is their private business – as though there is no requirement from God. You need to be in the body in order to know what your part is in the body. There are people professing to be in the body that are not in the body. They are trying to present that they have something to do but they are not doing it for the Lord because they are not in the body. When you are not in the body, the things of God mean nothing to you.

If you are not part of the body, do you care? Why doesn't it matter to you? Do you believe that you just "fake it 'til you make?" The purpose of sin is to show you that you are living by your flesh and to show you that you are being controlled by flesh.

Saved people are not flesh controlled, they are
Spirit controlled!

You can fool yourself into thinking you are in the
body of Christ because you don't live like you used
to. "I still do *little* sins, but I don't do the big ones!
I'm Okay!" The word of God seems difficult to you
because it is not talking to you. You must get in
the body first. The body of Christ is not human, it
is spiritual.

LIVE THE LIFE

"Now ye are the body of Christ, and members in particular." – I Corinthians 12:27

If you are not spiritual, how are you a part of the body of Christ? Get rid of the fallacy that being baptized in Jesus' name and speaking in tongues is how you remain saved! That is a part that you must do in order to get saved, but after that, you have to live the life! Yes, you were baptized but what are you doing now!

How do you know what your part is? It is spiritual. And as long as you deal with things in the flesh, you will never be able to perform in the body of Christ the way the Lord wants you to.

You can be a vessel of dishonor in the house. You may be used just to provoke others to make them see the need to get saved or to change. But that won't help you! If you are in the body, everything that is given to you to do is important.

WORK FOR THE BODY

*"For by one Spirit are we all baptized
into one body, whether we be Jews or
Gentiles, whether we be bond or free; and
have been all made to drink into one
Spirit."* – I Corinthians 12:13

You never argue or dispute the fact that because
you have ears, eyes, a nose, legs, feet, etc. that they
are a part of your body. Those things go together to
make up your body. You cannot be in the body of
Christ and work for other purposes. You must
work for the body. Even though there are many
different parts and functions of the body, it is still
only one body.

The way to get into the body is by being baptized –
being put to death with Jesus. You must be
baptized into the body whether you are a Jew or
Gentile. It does not matter what your background
or ethnicity is – we all must come into the body the
same way. No one gets in by some other means.
No one has an advantage or disadvantage because
of who they are or who they know. We get in by
being baptized into the body and we are introduced
into the body through the Holy Spirit.

Since flesh is not holy, how are you holy if you are
living after the flesh? The Lord is not trying to
save our flesh, for it will never be holy. He has

come to save us *from* our flesh. Consider this.
Whenever you have a problem, consider why you
are having the problem?   It's because of your flesh.

Unfortunately, many people's concept of salvation
has been wrong. They have come into salvation
because they want a better *human* life. They have
heard that by being saved they can have all those
things they could not have when they were in the
world. When you are in the body, you are part of
the body of Jesus. You should have no personal
views, works or vendettas. If your focus is only on
those things which are naturally beneficial, you
will never "set your affections on things above."
Salvation comes to benefit us spiritually, and only
by aligning ourselves with the Spirit, and by
walking *in* the Spirit, will we see the benefits in
every aspect of our lives!

MORTIFY THE DEEDS OF THE FLESH

"For if ye live after the flesh, ye shall die:
but if ye through the Spirit do mortify the
deeds of the body, ye shall live." –
Romans 8:13

Many people come into salvation and never stop
operating by their human mind. That is where the
problems come from. You end up right back where
you were before salvation, only now you are a
pretender! You pretend to be saved and you don't
want to acknowledge that you are not saved. If you
won't acknowledge that you are not really saved,
you will never be able to be saved.

If you are still conducting yourself according to
your human feelings, you know you are not
operating spiritually. The only way you will get to
be spiritual is to accept it. Sin shows you that you
are still partial to your flesh. Scripture says
mortify the deeds of the flesh. Make them inactive.
But you continue to feel justified reacting to things
that go against the flesh.

Everything that God allows to come to you is to
make you better not bitter! "It's coming against my
flesh and I don't like it!" Of course it is. That is
why it comes, to show you that you are still dealing
with flesh. When you are in the body, you are one
Spirit. You cannot come up with something

contrary to what you are being taught if you are of
the one Spirit.

BEING PART OF THE BODY

"For the body is not one member, but many." – I Corinthians 12:14

You know that your physical body is made up of many members, but it is only one body. In salvation, everything works by the one head/mind – Christ – even though there are many members. Where then do all these other ministries come from? How is Christ divided? They make people feel good about themselves...they are being "used" by God. It's a trick!

"If the foot shall say, Because I am not the hand, I am not of the body; is it therefore not of the body?"
– I Corinthians 12:15

He uses an obvious part of the body – the foot and hand. You would not have a complete body with just a foot or a hand. One part of the body can't feel less important because they are not the hand or the foot. You are a part of the body and you are important and it is important that you meet your responsibility. This is about what Jesus wants us to do. "Oh, I don't do that!" Since when did you get the kind of authority to decide what you will and will not do? People pick their own way (God will allow you to make the choice) and then they don't like the way they chose. "I thought I knew what I

wanted!" That's always a mistake, to follow what
you want. Now, you have to try to make whatever
you get what you want it to be. That' a tough job!

GOD SETS MEMBERS IN THE BODY

"If the whole body were an eye, where
were the hearing? If the whole were
hearing, where were the smelling?"
– I Corinthians 12:17

The human body has five senses to be able to detect
things in the natural. The senses are part of the
natural body. Not everybody processes taste the
same way. Some might eat something that is
delicious and some one else eats it and doesn't find
it appetizing. The ear is a part of the body, as are
the eye and the nose. All are part of the "human"
you. That is for the benefit of the human body.

The benefit of your spiritual body is the Holy
Ghost. We are to know no man after the flesh
anymore. Any revelation you get must come from
the Holy Ghost or it is not a spiritual revelation.

"But now hath God set the members every
one of them in the body, as it hath
pleased him." – I Corinthians 12:18

God sets the members in the body. Many want to
know what their gift is. They ask the pastor,
"What is my gift?" You need to be saved first.
What kind of gift are you going to operate in if you
are not saved? How will you help people spiritually

if you are not saved? Your main focus has become, "Why am I being treated like this? Why me?"

You have become your own idol. By dealing with your problems you acknowledge that you are more important than the Lord. But you are not the decision maker. Jesus is. Whatever he allows to come to you is for your benefit.

Once you acknowledge and allow God's control of your life, then His purpose for your life will unfold – your gift, indeed will make room for you.

WHERE ARE YOU NOW?

"And if they were all one member, where were the body?" – 1 Corinthians 12:19

The Lord has many members in his body. How do you get in the body of Christ? You are put to death. You are born again. When you were brought into the body, did you die? Did you get in through death?

There is no other way but through death. When you look at the truth of salvation, not many people are saved. And it doesn't seem to concern people that much that they are not saved. It's kind of like the belief in the "boogie man" – if I just cover up my head, he will go away! "If I just pretend like I'm saved, everything will be okay!" See where you are so you can get where you need to be.

SURRENDER TO THE LORD

"But now are they many members, yet but one body." – I Corinthians 12:20

All God wants is a surrendered person. Life is not about you. Your agenda is of no importance. The reason you have a problem with people saying things to you that you don't like is because you are not surrendered to God. Jesus did not act like the world. He wasn't like the world. Our job is to be like him – to surrender to Him. God is able to move you to the place in him to accomplish his purpose. You are not to try to work things out. Your job is to accept that it is already done. It's already worked out!

"Nay, much more those members of the body, which seem to be more feeble, are necessary." – I Corinthians 12:22

Most of the things you make a big deal out of, you can live without. You count things important. You spend a lot of time on it. It is something you can live without. Those parts that you say are more feeble, those are the parts that are necessary.

LOOKS ARE DECEIVING

"And those members of the body, which we think to be less honourable, upon these we bestow more abundant honour; and our uncomely parts have more abundant comeliness." – I Corinthians 12:23

As long as the devil can keep you tied up with your own petty problems, you will be neutralized and of no effect in the kingdom of God – *until the day you die!*

The scripture above is dealing with the body of Christ. Some people would go to hell just to be able to do what their flesh dictates to them as being important. We think that some things are more honorable and important than others.

God does not think the way we think. Even the person who just sits in the pew – who we may think of as "do nothings" (just because they come to church), God views them as honorable. The human heart, to look at it, is not a beautiful thing, is it? You would not want to do without it, however. It may not look good, but it is of great value to you!

SALVATION IS THE MAIN THING

*"That there should be no schism in the
body; but that the members should have
the same care one for another."
- I Corinthians 12:25*

Do your best to be submissive to what God wants.
You must accept what the Lord says. That is the
only thing that can help you. That is what makes
the difference. There are many things trying to get
your attention. Much of it will distract you and
cause you to have your mind on things other than
that which is spiritual. You must establish your
priorities. What are the most important things in
life? It better be that which is spiritual or you will
end up being hurt. Do your best to keep the main
thing – salvation and serving the Lord – the main
thing!

*"I exhort therefore, that, first of all,
supplications, prayers, intercessions, and
giving of thanks, be made for all men." –
I Timothy 2:1*

To exhort means to encourage. Do you encourage
others? If I tell you that you can live saved, you
can live free from sin, I am encouraging you. You
think if I join your "pity party" and agree with you,
that that is encouragement, but it is not!

Supplications, prayers... can you pray for someone
and make then change? No!

What is the purpose of prayer? It is to get you to
line up with God! Intercession is praying in behalf
of someone else. You are offering supplication
before the Lord so that the person can get more
help. How do you help them? By being spiritual –
meaning, directed by the Spirit.

NOTHING WILL CHANGE UNTIL YOU CHANGE

*"For kings, and for all that are in
authority; that we may lead a quiet and
peaceable life in all godliness and
honesty." – I Timothy 2:2*

You are to pray for the world leaders. Pray for
kings and all that are in authority across the world.
God has called us to a quiet and peaceful life.

You want to be able to lead a quiet and peaceful life
but, how can you do that when you allow your
imagination to tell you that others are out to get
you. Your imagination keeps you from living that
life. In order to help someone else, your thinking
must first change.

*"For this is good and acceptable in the
sight of God our Saviour." – I Timothy
2:3*

Your conduct towards other people is to be good
and acceptable in the sight of God. We are praying
and waiting for others to change. God is waiting
for you to change. This is not about someone else.
Nothing will change for you until you change. If
you don't trust God, you have nothing going for you.
Have you really helped a person if you don't help
them spiritually? Our priority is to get people

saved. That is the only thing that will help them. You can get them a degree, a PhD, food, shelter, but if they are not saved, they will still end up in hell!

GOD WILL HAVE ALL MEN TO BE SAVED

"Who will have all men to be saved, and
to come unto the knowledge of the truth."
– I Timothy 2:4

God will have all men to be saved. Will all men be
saved? It is not likely! But, it is God's will that all
men be saved. How can people come to the
knowledge of the Truth if Truth is not being
taught? How can one know what it means to be
saved and to live saved if it is not being taught?

We want to do that which does not cost us anything
– it does not cost you anything to shout. We will do
that all day long because it doesn't cost you
anything. Talk is cheap! Anybody can make noise.
But, God will have all men to be saved. You need
truth. It is the truth that sets men free. You can
only receive the truth through the Spirit.

FREEDOM FROM FLESH

"Who gave himself a ransom for all, to be testified in due time." – I Timothy 2:6

The thing that has us captured is our flesh. Jesus died to give us freedom from the flesh, not to cut down on doing things that humans do. If you are still doing things that humans do, you are still a sinner. You need to be saved! You will have joy in your life when you are saved.

> *"Whereunto I am ordained a preacher, and an apostle, (I speak the truth in Christ, and lie not;) a teacher of the Gentiles in faith and verity."*
> *– I Timothy 2:7*

Paul is saying "I am called and ordained to preach the gospel of salvation." If you are called to preach at all, that is what you are called to preach – the gospel of salvation. What is the benefit of any other gospel? The gospel is the death, burial and resurrection of Jesus for the purpose of you and I being buried and resurrected with him. That is the good news – he died for us and we are now dead with him! We are teachers of the gentile...teaching them in faith and proving that salvation works. It is not enough to tell people salvation works, they must see it!

SAVED BY CONDUCT

*"I will therefore that men pray every
where, lifting up holy hands, without
wrath and doubting." – I Timothy 2:8*

You are not to be double-minded. You can't say you
believe one minute and then fail to believe the next
minute. If you put things in the Lord's hands, you
will find out that they are already taken care of.
Men pray everywhere...there is always a need or
cause to be praying. If somebody is acting
unseemly, pray for them. So you will know how to
act when you interact with them.

When you pray, praying helps you. Lift up holy
hands. Don't do anything to defile your hands.
"But they did it first!" You have to be able to lift up
holy hands without wrath and double-mindedness.
You getting mad or hurt or disgruntled or
suspicious – does not help you with God.

*"In like manner also, that women adorn
themselves in modest apparel, with
shamefacedness and sobriety; not with
broided hair, or gold, or pearls, or costly
array." – I Timothy 2:9*

"Modest" is used in the sense of making sure that
you are fully covered – that you are not showing
any unnecessary parts. Understand that you are

saved by your conduct in life – not by what you wear or don't wear! You will be lost – not because you wear pants or cut your hair – but because you are not saved! What needs to be seen is good works from women professing godliness. When you are saved, you should be drawing people to the Lord because they see Christ in you – not because of your "hour glass figure."

REJECT THE UNGODLY LIFE

*"In like manner also, that women adorn
themselves in modest apparel, with
shamefacedness and sobriety; not with
broided hair, or gold, or pearls, or costly
array." – I Timothy 2:9*

The Bible warns us of things to come. It tells us
plainly to reject ungodly living. Who listens to
anyone who tells them those things that are
beneficial to them, today? People are disrespectful
and don't regard titles and who they argue with.
Those things that do not lead people to spirituality
are coming. It is the devil's job to deceive you. The
devil presents to you the things you want;
therefore, he can deceive you. It's his job to make
you believe you can have what you can't have, as
long as following after it leads you away from the
Lord.

Natural man can not see what is spiritual. Carnal
man is unable to deal with things spiritually. The
doctrine of the devil always appeals to your flesh.
As long as you are "feeding him flesh" the devil will
stay in your face. People act like they are saved,
but acting won't get you into heaven.

You have obtained from God all that you need to be
saved – pass it on. Men can always receive things
naturally. But, God wants you to receive and do

those things which are spiritual. If you are walking spiritually, you won't be a part of ungodly living and you may be able to help someone, spiritually.

JESUS WAS A WORKER

"Neither give heed to fables and endless genealogies, which minister questions, rather than godly edifying which is in faith: so do." – I Timothy 1:4

Speak those things that build people up – spiritually; not that which inflates their heads! Don't deal with false or misleading things, or genealogies, backgrounds, or ancestry. You are only somebody if you have been born again and are saved and serving God!

Otherwise, you are nothing. Your value is only beneficial if you are serving God. Outside of him, you are worthless – worth less! Jesus was a worker. He worked. It does not matter who your mother was or what your background is. Can you work?

CHARITY IS LOVE IN ACTION

*"Now the end of the commandment is
charity out of a pure heart, and of a good
conscience, and of faith unfeigned." – I
Timothy 1:5*

Love fulfills the commandment of God. Charity is
love in action! It's love out of a pure heart –
without ulterior motive. It is without added
mixture – pure. It means operating for the purpose
of God with a pure heart. What good is feigned
faith? When you exercise faith, it gets larger. The
reason yours is mall is because you don't use it.

We go from faith to faith. When we see the Lord
operate in one situation, we have faith to believe
when the next situation arises. When you show
love, you don't need a commandment. You cannot
show God's love without having salvation. There
are different types of love. Agape is the love of God.
His love does not discriminate. He loves in spite of.
Faith is true faith – not pretend or feigned faith.
You see what God has done when you exercise faith
in him. Believe that God has done it – whatever
you need.

THE LAW IS FOR THE LAWLESS

*"Desiring to be teachers of the law;
understanding neither what they say, nor
whereof they affirm." – I Timothy 1:7*

The law is spiritual and it cannot be followed by
human beings. Israel had the law over 4,000 years
and could not keep it. The law is spiritual and is
kept by faith. You cannot live a saved life without
Jesus. He must direct us daily. When you live in
the Spirit, you will do what is spiritual all the time.

*"But we know that the law is good, if a
man use it lawfully." – I Timothy 1:8*

The law is good – how can it bring death? It is good
if it is used lawfully. A person that is saved does
not need a law telling them what he can and cannot
do because he is not going to break the law. If you
are saved, you are not going to break the law.

*"Knowing this, that the law is not made
for a righteous man, but for the lawless
and disobedient, for the ungodly and for
sinners, for unholy and profane, for
murderers of fathers and murderers of
mothers, for manslayers..." – I Timothy
1:9*

134

The law is for the lawless, not for the righteous. If you are righteous, you don't need a law. The law is for the disobedient, ungodly, sinners, unholy, profane, murderers, manslayers, etc. Saved people don't do wrong.

BISHOPS MUST BE BLAMELESS

"A bishop then must be blameless, the husband of one wife, vigilant, sober, of good behaviour, given to hospitality, apt to teach." – I Timothy 3:2

You desire a good work if you desire the office of a bishop. But, everyone is not cut out to be a bishop, even though they may desire it. Bishops must be blameless. In other words, when he is brought before the church, he must not have problems that people can bring against him. He must be found without blame if he is to fill that position.

Bishops must be the husband of one wife. He must be vigilant – you don't want someone who has no zeal or determination to do anything. Many don't want to do anything, they just want the title. Anything that seems to mean something, "Give me the title so it sounds like I am something!"

He must be sober and of good behavior; given to hospitality and be a person who can entreat people kindly. There are preachers who cannot do that. Some can be very mean and hateful.

Bishops must be apt to teach. Many have a ministry built on preaching and stirring people, but they cannot teach them. They keep people emotionally stirred but the people are "word hungry" because they are not being fed, spiritually.

BISHOPS HAVE A TOUGH JOB

"One that ruleth well his own house, having his children in subjection with all gravity." – I Timothy 3:4

Bishops have a tough job on their hands. He must rule well his own house. The only way it is possible to do this is to put things in the hands of the Lord. You cannot a make anyone do anything! All who have not found that out as of yet, will!

"I am the head!" What does that mean, today? It means you are to go before the family; you go ahead of them and act as a shield. "Having his children in subjection with all gravity." All that is within his power to do, he must do. He cannot shirk his responsibility. You must do what you are required to do.

THE WAY THEY SHOULD GO

"Train up a child in the way he should go: and when he is old, he will not depart from it." – Proverbs 22:6

By the time children are 4 or 5, their attitudes are already set. How they will conduct themselves is already set! If you wait until then to correct them, you are too late! We think the things they do as toddlers are cute ("He told me to shut up!") But when he is doing it at 15, that is another story! Children need to learn respect and how to accept discipline at an early age.

NOT BY FORCE, NOT BY MIGHT

"For if a man know not how to rule his own house, how shall he take care of the church of God? – I Timothy 3:5

How do you rule the church of God? Can the pastor take his belt to us? Can he hit us with a switch? Taking care of the church of God must be done spiritually. If you think you can do it by force, you have missed it. If you think you can run your house by force, you have missed it. Have you found that out, yet? We like to think we can take charge and do something. But, that is not the case in salvation. Children will act like they will obey until they are out of your sight!

The kids are just like us! We do right as long as we think someone is looking. There is not much difference between them and us! We think "Boy, these kids are terrible!" But, they are a reflection of us. Your children are a product of you. You think "What happened to them?!" The most you can do is pray that in a few years they will undergo a change.

In the household and in the church, we need to be available to help. Many times we have a belief about a situation and the kids see the same thing and have a totally different "take" on it. We think, because we are adults, that we are right! When you tell children they are wrong all the time, they start to have a problem with it.

GODLINESS IS A MYSTERY

"And without controversy great is the
mystery of godliness: God was manifest
in the flesh, justified in the Spirit, seen of
angels, preached unto the Gentiles,
believed on in the world, received up into
glory." – I Timothy 3:16

Great is the mystery of God. God was manifest in
flesh. God is a Spirit, so he had to put on a body of
flesh so that men would be able to know him
outside of the abstract. If God were a man, Jesus is
what he would be. But he is not a man. God was
justified in the Spirit – this is done spiritually.
That creates a puzzle for us – how to grasp what is
spiritual. If you try to grasp it by human means,
you take away from it spiritually. The only way to
get what is spiritual is by faith.

It is by faith and not by what you do. " I accept
what God says." How difficult is that? "If I don't
see it, if I don't understand it, how am I supposed
to accept it?" Do you ever accept anything that you
don't see? If you have to understand what God says
first, you are stuck. If you cannot accept what God
says, the best thing to do is get a heat resistant suit
and get ready to make it to the lake!

Your problem is being a human being. That is
what God saved you from. Why go back and keep

on being human? Your fleshly nature is your enemy. We want to be saved through our human intellect rather than through the Spirit of God – it will never work! God was "seen of angels, preached unto the gentiles, believed on in the world and received up into glory." We must accept it by faith, even though "I don't know how it works" – just accept it!"

A SEED MUST DIE TO GIVE LIFE

*"For if we have been planted together in
the likeness of his death, we shall be also
in the likeness of his resurrection." –
Romans 6:5*

You cannot be born again unless you die. A seed
must die in order to give life! We don't come into
salvation believing that we are going to be a
different person than what we were. If you try to
improve on what you were, you would only be more
of what you were – not different from what you
were.

You were resurrected to a new life, not a better life
for you, but to a new life in Christ. You cannot be
"rehabbed." You have to be born again. Until you
are new, you are not better. Until you are put to
death, you are still the same.

OLD THINGS ARE PASSED AWAY

*"And, being assembled together with
them, commanded them that they should
not depart from Jerusalem, but wait for
the promise of the Father, which, saith
he, ye have heard of me." – Acts 1:4*

Why do we resist change? Why don't we want to be
spiritual? Do you have too much fun being a
human being? "I want God to change things and
make things better for me but I don't want to
change!"

He said "Wait for the promise of the father." God
came to make us spiritual beings – born of the
water and of the Spirit. We now exist to glorify the
Lord. Our life is about pleasing him and doing
what he saved us to do. It is not about what "I
want and what I am trying to accomplish." You
hinder your blessing by getting too busy trying to
get what you want and not what God has for you.
If you don't want what God has for you, how will
you get it?

*"For John truly baptized with water; but
ye shall be baptized with the Holy Ghost
not many days hence." – Acts 1:5*

Paul let them know that they would be baptized
with the Holy Ghost. The purpose of the baptism is

145

to become directed by the Spirit. Baptism
represents being put to death with Jesus, that is,
being buried with him. You are united with him by
being put to death with him. Old things are passed
away.

POWER TO LIVE SAVED

*"But ye shall receive power, after that the
Holy Ghost is come upon you: and ye
shall be witnesses unto me both in
Jerusalem, and in all Judaea, and in
Samaria, and unto the uttermost part of
the earth." – Acts 1:8*

Ye shall receive power. What kind of power?
Power to live saved. When you do not recognize
what you have received, how can it help you? We
get stuck on "I spoke in tongues!" – not the fact that
"I got saved from myself." Flesh is your enemy
because flesh is determined to keep you living to
satisfy it!

After the Holy Ghost comes upon you, you are to
witness for the Lord. Your life becomes a witness.
If you never open your mouth to tell anyone you
have the Holy Ghost, you will still be a witness.
We witness with our life, not with our mouths.
Your life is a greater testimony that what you say.

TONGUES OF FIRE

*"And when the day of Pentecost was fully
come, they were all with one accord in
one place. And suddenly there came a
sound from heaven as of a rushing
mighty wind, and it filled all the house
where they were sitting." – Acts 2:1-2*

As they were on one accord, what happened? There
came a sound from heaven as a rushing mighty
wind. A sound is different from the actual wind,
even if it is the wind making the sound. It did not
say there "came a *wind* from heaven," but a *sound*.
The sound was as though it was rushing past
something. And it – the sound – filled all the house
where they were sitting. The sound filled the
house. Everyone in the house heard the sound.

*"And there appeared unto them cloven
tongues like as of fire, and it sat upon
each of them." – Acts 2:3*

There appeared unto them cloven tongues.
"Appeared" means it became apparent. Things can
become apparent by other senses than eyesight.
You distinguish something by other means than
sight. You can smell, taste, and feel things. You
know that popcorn is in the room by the smell,
whether you see it popping or not. There appeared
– became apparent to them – cloven or divided

tongues. The tongues referred to are actually languages – not physical tongues! And it is not a real fire. "Like as" indicates that it had similar qualities as fire does – it purged them. When you receive the Holy Ghost, you are purged from the life you have been living. You have been purged from being a fleshly person. The languages "sat" – or, rested – on each of them and they all spoke with tongues. We get stuck on the tongues rather than focus on what the Holy Ghost came to do.

THE GIFT OF GOD

"Then Peter said unto them, Repent, and be baptized every one of you in the name of Jesus Christ for the remission of sins, and ye shall receive the gift of the Holy Ghost." – Acts 2:38

Peter told them to repent – turn from your wicked ways, do an about face, reverse what you have been doing and be buried/baptized – everyone of you in the name of Jesus Christ for the remission or taking away of sin. "And you shall receive the gift of the Holy Ghost."

They had to be made aware that the Holy Ghost was a gift. You did not get him because you tarried or knew how to say "Jesus" rapidly. He was a gift to you from Jesus Christ.

If you are willing to submit your life to him and live for him, he will give you the Holy Ghost. People get the Holy Ghost for themselves. But when you receive the Holy Ghost you become a servant of the Lord. We get saved so that things will go better for "me." We believe that "Now that I am saved, things should go my way!" Should they? We come in to salvation looking for something for our self rather than coming into serve the Lord. We forget that we are *his* servant – he is not here to serve us!

TRUTH IS THE STANDARD

*"Hold fast the form of sound words,
which thou hast heard of me, in faith and
love which is in Christ Jesus." – II
Timothy 1:13*

Truth is the standard. And most don't want to deal
with truth. The truth is what God operates by, so
why not follow what God is doing to benefit you?
The truth is how you get what God has made
available for you.

If you don't know the truth, how will you get what
God has made available? The way to get what God
has made available to his people is to know the
truth. "If I know the truth, then I must start to live
a spiritual life. So I stay away from truth. I blame
the devil when things happen!"

You are not getting what you could have. You are
not doing what God requires you to do. You are not
following the standard. Hold fast sound words.
How do you determine what are sound words?
Sound words work! The word of God is truth and it
works when you do what it says. God says "If you
love me, you will keep my commandments." If you
are obedient to God's word, it will benefit you.

ĎO IT GOD'S WAY

Humans want to feel like "I did it my way!" To some, that is more important than pleasing God. You cannot serve two masters. If you love yourself, then that is who you will serve. Humans love themselves. That is why you must be born again! You cannot, of yourself, do what God requires. "But how do I live saved?" You cannot do it yourself. Jesus is the only one who knows how to do it. You must rely on him. As a human being, you are always looking for what you have to do! "I have some part to play in this, right?" No, salvation is by faith. I accept what Jesus has already done. If something is done, what is your part to do? Nothing! There is no salvation outside of Jesus. "I say I trust Jesus, even though I prove all of the time that I only trust myself!"

The tendency of God's people is to deal with things from a human standpoint – trying to handle things ourselves. Until you realize this, you won't get very far in salvation. You continue to think that someone else is creating your problem. No one else is your problem – only you!

> *"Paul, an apostle of Jesus Christ by the will of God, according to the promise of life which is in Christ Jesus..."*
> *– II Timothy 1:1*

Whatever goes on in your life once you are saved is by the will of God. This seems difficult to accept for many. "You mean when they lie on me, cheat on me, do me wrong, etc. it is the will of God?" Why does God allow these types of things to happen to good people? Because God wants those good people to be saved! If you are handling things naturally, you are not spiritual. He allows those things to come to show you that – when you react to situations – you are operating by flesh and not the Spirit.

LIFE IS IN JESUS

*"Paul, an apostle of Jesus Christ by the
will of God, according to the promise of
life which is in Christ Jesus..."*
– II Timothy 1:1

Life is in Christ Jesus. We come alive by being
dead with him! "How am I supposed to be dead
when people are messing with me? I don't like it!"
Why would God allow these things to happen? If he
did not, how would he impress upon you that life in
him is spiritual?

When the Lord starts trying to get your attention,
you think something is going wrong. Yes, it's you
that is going wrong. He is trying to get you back on
the right track! "I think I can be saved if I can only
get people in this world to treat me the way I want
to be treated – then I can be saved!" That is not
how this world operates. It is set up to cause you to
see your problem.

As long as you look at things from a human
standpoint, you will always be mystified by the
spiritual. When you accept the things of God by
faith, you will find out that it works and that it is
guaranteed to work – according to the promise of
life. Jesus is the one who promises life. If Jesus is
not in your life, you have no spiritual life.

ONLY BY FAITH

"I thank God, whom I serve from my
forefathers with pure conscience, that
without ceasing I have remembrance of
thee in my prayers night and day."
– II Timothy 1:3

When you are praying for someone, what do you
accomplish for them? What do you accomplish for
God? Praying is for you. Fasting is for you. We
have been misled to believe that praying changes
God or changes other people. But the truth is that
praying is to change you! When you are praying,
you are acknowledging the problem and so you
must now interact with the person or situation,
acknowledging that they have a problem.
And once you acknowledge that the person has a
problem, you make the change and operate
spiritually with them. Praying for someone does
not have to change them – it should change you.

"When I call to remembrance the
unfeigned faith that is in thee, which
dwelt first in thy grandmother Lois, and
thy mother Eunice; and I am persuaded
that in thee also." – II Timothy 1:5

What does he mean by "unfeigned faith"? Many
have pretend faith. How do you know whether or
not you believe God? If you believe God, you

conduct yourself as though it has already happened. It is done! We are creatures of sight – "I must see it first!" If you believe only what you can see, you are not operating in faith. You don't have to understand it. If God says it is true, you accept it. You cannot walk on water until you get out of the ship!

THE AFFLICTIONS OF THE GOSPEL

"Be not thou therefore ashamed of the testimony of our Lord, nor of me his prisoner: but be thou partaker of the afflictions of the gospel according to the power of God." – II Timothy 1:8

Affliction is another word saints don't like. The afflictions of the Gospel – you are going to go through hardship because of your promotion of the gospel. Don't be ashamed of God. You are just making your investment and the return is going to come back to you later. People are ashamed of the Lord's testimony. What did Jesus go through?

You haven't suffered anything near what Jesus suffered! Don't be ashamed because you are a prisoner for the Lord. You may be accused of being guilty of something, but don't be ashamed. There is power available for you when you are going through your tests and trials. If you are not saved in the test, you are not saved! The next time the test and trials come along, you will fail if you approach them any other way than spiritually. Some people have in their mind that there are just some things they will not allow people to do to them. They build themselves up to be so important that they are willing to risk everything to get even with anyone who opposes or offends them.

"Who hath saved us, and called us with an holy calling, not according to our works, but according to his own purpose and grace, which was given us in Christ Jesus before the world began." – II Timothy 1:9

God called us to be holy. Why do you say you are saved if you are not living holy? "I thought if I worked in the church that it counts for something!" Thank God that salvation is not according to our works.

IN UNION WITH CHRIST

"Who hath saved us, and called us with
an holy calling, not according to our
works, but according to his own purpose
and grace, which was given us in Christ
Jesus before the world began."
– II Timothy 1:9

You get the benefit of what the Lord has by being
in union with him. You have to be a "union" man!
If you are not in (the) union, you don't get the
benefits. Everything was in him before the world
began. So, when you accept him and are in union
with him, you have everything that he has. Beware
of an "individualized salvation"...laid out for you
alone. Fleshly men want a "tailor-made" salvation
made to fit their own ideas and plans.

However, before the world existed, God already had
everything planned. You must line up with his
plan or you will not benefit from it.

"But is now made manifest by the
appearing of our Saviour Jesus Christ,
who hath abolished death, and hath
brought life and immortality to light
through the gospel." – II Timothy 1:10

Until the Jesus showed up on the scene, we could
not experience salvation. We could read about it,

hear about it; but, it was not available. There is no more death for you once you accept salvation. You died once by dying to flesh. That is your death! Your entire future depends upon you being dead to your flesh. Death is a transition to the spiritual state.

BROUGHT INTO LIFE

"But is now made manifest by the appearing of our Saviour Jesus Christ, who hath abolished death, and hath brought life and immortality to light through the gospel." – II Timothy 1:10

We have now been brought into life! You thought when you were out there in the world "partying" you were really living! But you had no life. When you breathed your first breath, you were on your way to hell. But, now that you are born again, death has been abolished. You don't have to worry about it anymore. You became immortal once you were born again. What does that mean? You now have eternal life, and that which is eternal remains for ever. You will never change; you will always be able to be in the presence of the Lord.

Jesus brought before us that which we can have when we are in union with Christ. Light is revelation. Why do we need revelation? You need light to illuminate what is going on and to see what is actually true in the room. The Holy Spirit is the light that reveals to us what is spiritual. Humans are not trying to find out what is spiritual. They want something revealed that humans can understand.

God deals with spiritual revelation. When you accept what is spiritual it will revolutionize your life. When you determine "I am going to accept everything that God says," everything about you will change. The Holy Ghost comes to reveal things that are spiritual so you can live a life in the spirit.

How do you know when you are spiritual? You will know by whether or not you have a problem with the things that come against your natural life.

FLESH CANNOT CHANGE

*"But she that liveth in pleasure is dead
while she liveth." – I Timothy 5:6*

The person that is looking for something for
themselves is already dead because they are living
their life for the flesh; they are not committed to
that which is spiritual. Without a commitment to
that which is spiritual, there is no way you will be
saved. No one can be saved naturally.

*"And these things give in charge, that
they may be blameless." – I Timothy 5:7*

The minute you start dealing with things
spiritually, all that God has revealed to you will be
brought back to your memory. The reason that it
does not work otherwise is because knowing what
God says as a human, what could you do about it?
Humans cannot do what God says. If you are
fleshly minded, when pressure comes upon you, you
will revert back to reacting as human being. Flesh
cannot change. Flesh always remains flesh. You
become dead to living after flesh through accepting
the death of the Lord. You must accept his death
and cease living after flesh.

THE WAY OF FAITH

"But if any provide not for his own, and specially for those of his own house, he hath denied the faith, and is worse than an infidel." – I timothy 5:8

You may be proclaiming to trust in God, but you are not conducting yourself as though you know him if you don't provide for your household. You ought to do your part to take care of your siblings and those in your charge. Otherwise, you are worse than a person who never confessed to believe in God.

Salvation is called the way faith. You are to be a believer in salvation. If you are out of faith, where are you spiritually? Spirituality and faith are the same. You access the things the Lord has for you by faith. It's already done. The way to access what you need is by faith!

WORTHY OF DOUBLE HONOR

"Let the elders that rule well be counted worthy of double honour, especially they who labour in the word and doctrine." – I Timothy 5:17

Do you think the Lord is really concerned about oxen or did he say this because of his concern for the ministry? You cannot put a restriction on the delivery of the Word of God. You cannot muzzle the person who is preaching the Word. You cannot restrict him from preaching what he is told by God to preach. If you don't believe the word, you have no hope.

If you honor the elders, then you are to give double honor to those that rule well. They that labor in the word and doctrine are worthy of double honor. Many people who represent the ministry today are caught up in hype and emotions, stirring people's feelings – "Money cometh!" – "It's in the mail!" – "Step on the devil's head" – "Kick the devil out!"

Many preachers try to deal with the word diplomatically so that they don't offend people. But, if you are afraid to offend people, you will not be able to help them. The truth, though it may hurt, liberates!

CHRISTIANITY IS A WAY OF LIFE

*"If any man teach otherwise, and consent
not to wholesome words, even the words
of our Lord Jesus Christ, and to the
doctrine which is according to godliness."*
– I Timothy 6:3

If anyone teaches anything other than the word of
God, it is for the purpose of deception. They want
to deceive you. They add enough word to make you
believe that it is what God said; but, they add in
their own personal touch. A little lie is all lie!
They add the scripture to deceive you and set you
up to believe the lie. So, you will say, "Its'
according to scripture." If you don't know scripture,
you won't know that what was said is not scripture.

Beware of how they word is presented to you.
When you hear that you are going to get all these
blessings without you having to change your
lifestyle – don't trust it! The point of teaching is to
build up the faith of the believer. Scripture will
back itself up. Anything that teaches you that you
don't have to live godly is not of God.

THE CORRUPT MIND

"Perverse disputings of men of corrupt minds, and destitute of the truth, supposing that gain is godliness: from such withdraw thyself." – I Timothy 6:5

All humans are prideful. Men of corrupt minds are perverse. Every one who thinks naturally is of a corrupt mind. Their thoughts will not stand and are certain to change. A wavery-minded man gets nothing from the Lord because, one minute he thinks in behalf of God, and the next he will not trust Him. With God you have to trust him and stick with it.

Some people, being right on the verge of blessing, give up just before God blesses them! "I'm tired!" We believe that great gain is godliness, not the other way around. We equate salvation with what God blesses us with. True – God wants you to have financial blessings; but the way you get it is by sowing unto the Lord! That is His plan. The moment you start believing what God says, you will begin receiving the blessing that he has for you. But if you waver, how will get it?

GODLINESS WITH CONTENTMENT

"But godliness with contentment is great gain. For we brought nothing into this world, and it is certain we can carry nothing out." – I Timothy 6:6-7

These statements are addressed to spiritual people. If you are saved, you are content. Learn to live with and learn to live without. Godliness with contentment is great gain. When you came here you didn't have a thing –not even a suit of clothes. Now, all of a sudden, you become so important but when you leave you take nothing with you. You are here to prepare yourself to spend an eternity with God. Many are so caught up in their own personal lives they don't take time to witness for the Lord.

"And having food and raiment let us be therewith content." – I Timothy 6:8

You have food. You have clothing. You have shelter. Why can't you be satisfied? Be happy with the necessities of life that God has provided.

IN GOD WE TRUST

*"But they that will be rich fall into
temptation and a snare, and into many
foolish and hurtful lusts, which drown
men in destruction and perdition."*
– I Timothy 6:9

Being rich does not have to be a problem in
salvation. What seems to happen is that people
begin to trust in their riches rather than in the God
that blessed them to have it. You must still trust
God even though you have much. Often, the
wealthy fall into temptation and are snared. They
start to act like they are God and start to feel their
"power." When you feel like you can use money to
control things and people, you are in trouble. You
cannot control God, and controlling people will not
help you. You need to surrender to the Lord.

"...Many foolish and hurtful lusts...." As long as
your mindset is to please your flesh, you will
eventually self-destruct! Many have hurt
themselves with many sorrows because they are
seeking money. Money is a necessity but it is not
more important than salvation. You can never put
money before your salvation. Serving God is top
priority at all times. When you serve God, He will
take care of you. He is still the supplier of all your
needs.

JESUS CAME TO SAVE US

*"But thou, O man of God, flee these
things; and follow after righteousness,
godliness, faith, love, patience,
meekness." – I Timothy 6:11*

Righteousness, godliness, faith, love, patience and
meekness – these are the things you want to follow
after. These things come through submitting
yourself to God and allowing him to control your
life. When you are in control, you are not being
controlled by the Lord. If you are being controlled
by your flesh, you are lost. He came to die so he
could save us. He will fight your battles for you.
Do not promote yourself and make yourself of more
importance than you really are. Jesus is important
– not you!

*"Fight the good fight of faith, lay hold on
eternal life, whereunto thou art also
called, and hast professed a good
profession before many witnesses."
– I Timothy 6:12*

Fight the good fight of faith. The battle ground is in
the spiritual realm. Faith and spiritual are one in
the same. That takes us out of the natural real to
deal with that which is spiritual. Nothing is ever to
be dealt with as just being something fleshly.
Everything in your life is spiritual, once you are

saved. Lay hold on eternal life by faith. You don't get it by works. It is not by what you can do. Faith says it is already done! It's human to think "I've got to get my hands on it and work it out myself!" Jesus came to save us – from us!

FLEE YOUTHFUL LUSTS

"Flee also youthful lusts: but follow righteousness, faith, charity, peace, with them that call on the Lord out of a pure heart." – II Timothy 2:22

Flee youthful lusts. Does that just mean youths are to flee these lusts? No, the commandment is also directed to older people. Substitute righteousness for youthful lusts. Follow faith, charity, peace – get away from those things that will lead you away from the Lord. Occupy your time with doing what is right – that which is in right standing with God.

People get caught up in what does and does not please them. They think they have a right to determine or pursue what they think will make them happy. It's a trick! Whatever you do, do it for the Lord. Stop being selfish! Salvation is not about you.

KNOWLEDGE PUFFS UP

"Now as touching things offered unto idols, we know that we all have knowledge. Knowledge puffeth up, but charity edifieth." – I Corinthians 8:1

Knowledge inflates your ego and makes you think you have attained something of value. What did you know when you were born into the world? Nothing. You had to learn from someone. When you went to grade school, you did not argue with your teacher – "No, one and one is not two!" But, when you come into salvation, you want to dispute the word of God.

We want the human knowledge/process we experienced to account for something in salvation. What is spiritual is the only thing of value. Everything you gained, you gained it. And it puffs you up. It makes you feel that you are somebody. Get the highest degree you can get, but don't allow the degree to control you! Don't allow things you learned human-wise to take priority over God's knowledge. All a man can know is known through his five senses. You cannot teach humans spiritual things. Spiritual things are spiritually discerned. They are not received by the five senses. Spiritual things do not agree with what is natural. When you are a fleshly-minded person, you do not want to hear what is spiritual. It takes away your pride. "If any man loves God, the same is known of him."

It is difficult to get the human mind to deflate itself. The scripture says that Jesus made himself of no reputation. Yet, man makes himself of reputation! What you think you know determines how you live your life.

GOD KNOWS THOSE THAT LOVE HIM

*"As concerning therefore the eating of
those things that are offered in sacrifice
unto idols, we know that an idol is
nothing in the world, and that there is
none other God but one."*
– I Corinthians 8:4

People have a problem with having to change their
view of something. When you come up with some
knowledge, you are "always right." God knows
those that love him. How? They obey him. If you
don't keep his commandments, stop lying to
yourself and thinking you love him. God has let us
know that knowledge puffs a person up. What you
think you know is not important, it is not reality.

Anything offered unto idols doesn't really mean
anything because an idol is not a god. But to the
person who believes that an idol means something,
his conscience is defiled. You have knowledge. You
know an idol is nothing. Don't offend the weak
brother by viewing what he sees as wrong even
though you know it is not wrong.

The title "god" is attached to many different names.
People make gods of themselves, spouses, children,
etc. Who do you obey? Whatever you obey becomes
your master. You cannot operate by what you

believe you know. There are many things you can make a god out of, but there is only one True God.

YOU CAUSE YOUR OWN PROBLEMS

*"Know ye not that the unrighteous shall
not inherit the kingdom of God? Be not
deceived: neither fornicators, nor
idolaters, nor adulterers, nor effeminate,
nor abusers of themselves with mankind;
Nor thieves, nor covetous, nor drunkards,
nor revilers, nor extortioners, shall
inherit the kingdom of God."
– I Corinthians 6:9–10*

You cause problems for yourself. If you realize it,
you could stop your problems by not doing what you
do to cause them! To stop the kicking, move out of
the way or quit pulling the rope! You are solely
responsible for whether your situation changes.
When you change, everything changes.

When you get involved in what God is doing, you
stop the progress because you find a way to take
the praise. God said he will give his glory to no
one. We are cautious of each other because we
think people are our problem! If you look in the
mirror you will see the real problem – You! Stop
deceiving yourself! You will do all that you can to
keep from allowing someone to deceive you; but you
will deceive yourself because you trust yourself,
even though you know you cannot be trusted!

JESUS IS THE ONLY WAY OUT

Human beings are looking for the easy way out – they do not want to tax their flesh in any way. "I don't have to live right but I just want to come and jump and shout and God's going to accept that without me changing my lifestyle!" But God requires a lifestyle change. Human beings cannot go to heaven. In order to get to heaven you have to be dead to living after your flesh. Something has got to get your attention to get you to the place where God wants you. If salvation was based on you doing anything (shouting, praying, etc.) it would not be based on faith in Jesus. People in the church have the wrong concept of salvation. Many think that doing *things* make you saved – if I pray, sing, shout, usher, etc. – I am saved. But, salvation is based on not living after flesh.

Human beings' major concern is themselves. What I don't want. What I don't like. Why I won't let anyone treat me like that. I want what I want, when I want it! Basically, humans are selfish. That is the nature of flesh. The nature of the watermelon is in the seed. The nature of the human is in the seed. You cannot train a watermelon to do anything but be a watermelon. You cannot train a human being to be anything but a human! That is why you must be born again with a new nature.

We always, as humans, look for the thing that allows us to do the most according to our fleshly nature. We want salvation to have something to do with what we do. But, it is about what Jesus has done; so it has to be by faith and not by human works or effort. You will never be able to do enough as a human to be saved. If salvation is by works, you wouldn't need faith! Israel was given the law and they could not keep it. God was trying to show them that they could not live for him as human beings. To live for God, you must be spiritual.

BORN AGAIN

We were not born in the final state that God
intended for man. Flesh is flawed. Jesus Christ
was born without sin, and committed no sin. He
alone, therefore, was able to die for the sins of the
world, being sinless Himself. By His example of
living sin–free while in a body of flesh, he
condemned sin in the flesh.

If you live after flesh, you are under condemnation.
However, Jesus, through his death, not only
brought the condemnation, but secured the means
by which you could be *free* from that condemnation.
By baptism you are put to death with him that you
might live according to the Spirit. This is obviously
not something you can do since you don't know how
to do it. But this is where faith steps in. For only
God could give you the power to live free from sin.

On the cross Jesus cried, "It is finished!" You don't
have to do anything but accept what the Lord has
already completed. Accept it by faith! We walk by
faith and not by sight. Faith says, "I don't have to
understand it. It does not have to make sense to
me. But I'll do it because God says so."

It is only after we accept Christ's death and life
that we come into the fullness of God's creation.
We are no longer fleshly–motivated human beings;
we have become spiritual beings, directed by His

Spirit alone. Only then can God look at us, His creation, and declare "that's good!"

TOPICAL INDEX

D

E

F

T

U – Z